Daily Life in People's China

Daily Life in People's China

ARTHUR W. GALSTON
with
JEAN S. SAVAGE

THOMAS Y. CROWELL COMPANY
New York Established 1834

Photograph facing page 1 by Audrey Topping.

Manufactured in the United States of America

ISBN 0–690–23140–7

1 2 3 4 5 6 7 8 9 10

Library of Congress Cataloging in Publication Data

Galston, Arthur William, 1920–
  Daily Life in People's China.

  Bibliography: p.
  1. China—Description and travel—1949
I. Title.   2-6-74
DS711.G34 1973   915.1'03'5   73–8776
ISBN 0–690–23140–7

To my friends, the peasants of the Marco Polo Bridge People's Commune: their gracious hospitality, unfailing good humor, and enormous capacity for sustained cooperative labor signal hope for the future of man.

Contents

Preface

EVERYWHERE I WENT in China, I recorded my immediate impressions by scribbling shorthand notes into a spiral notebook kept in my shirt pocket. Each night I reviewed these cryptic notes, organized a bit, and read them into a dictating machine. On being mailed back to the United States, the dictated belts were converted into diaries for both my 1971 and 1972 trips by my faithful and understanding secretary, Anna Francesconi, to whom all praise is due. In the fall of 1972, Jean Savage and I talked over the diaries and planned a book based on them. I prepared the first draft and reedited the final manuscript; she did all the hard organizational work in between. Almost every page shows some effect of her research, rewriting, and style editing.

I took all the photographs with a Pentax Spotmatic 35-mm camera on Kodak Ektachrome film. The transparencies were skillfully converted into black-and-white prints by the Davenport Custom Laboratory in Hamden, Connecticut.

I am grateful to the Josiah Macy Jr. Foundation for a grant which supported the recording and typing of the original notes, especially on medicine, science and education.

Although my wife and daughter are not coauthors, they have contributed to this book in many ways. Their opinions and impressions, frequently different from mine, helped me take a second look and avoid many easy generalizations. My daughter's own diary supplied many missing details and useful factual checks.

A note on pronunciation: I have adopted a system in which *ch'* is pronounced as in *cheese, ch* as in *Joe, p'* as in *peach, p* as in *beer; t'* as in *tennis,* and *t* as in *door.* This will not satisfy either the purists or the pragmatists, but I think it works.

Interest in the People's Republic of China runs high just now among Americans and other Westerners—a promising first step toward our improved understanding of China. It is to this end that the experiences and thoughts recounted in this book have been directed.

Daily Life in People's China

Old friends welcomed Ethan Signer (left) and the author to China in 1971. In Shanghai it was Dr. Loo Shih-wei of the Academia Sinica's Institute of Plant Physiology.

1

To China by Soybean

T H I S B O O K about China is not the work of a China expert or even a longtime China-watcher. It is rather an account of the sights, sounds, and feel of life in China today, recorded by an American scientist fortunate enough to be the first admitted to the People's Republic of China since its founding in 1949.

How did I gain entry into China at a time when so many others, better qualified by knowledge and experience, tried and failed? The answer is sufficiently eccentric to satisfy the most fatalistic reader. It began with soybeans—one of China's most useful contributions to agriculture in the United States. As a graduate student in biology in the 1940s, I had discovered that dilute sprays of a compound called 2,3-5 triiodobenzoic acid, or TIBA, could produce a tenfold increase in the number of flower buds, and subsequently of harvestable pods, on soybean plants. Higher concentrations led to serious malformations of the plant, including shedding of leaves and buds. Having duly noted these facts in my Ph.D. dissertation, I went into the service in 1943, ultimately serving as Agriculture Officer for the United States Naval Military Government in Okinawa. I learned only several years later of the unanticipated consequences of my work with TIBA.

After a certain amount of commercial exploitation to increase soybean crop yields in the American Midwest, TIBA had been developed for military use as a defoliant at the United States Army Chemical Corps Laboratories in Fort Detrick, Maryland. Although TIBA itself was never used by the military, two related chemicals, 2,4-D and 2,4,5-T, were developed into potent weapons and used extensively in Indochina. During the decade starting in 1961, more than one hundred million pounds of these materials were sprayed over an area of more than six million acres. Such a gigantic chemical warfare effort was unprecedented, and the effects on the ecology and the people of Vietnam are still largely unknown.

All too late, scientists and other concerned Americans began to react to the staggering implications of their country's actions in Vietnam. My own disquietude focused on my unforeseen connections with the origin of a weapon that might be contributing to the ecological destruction of a small Southeast Asian country. I joined a group of other American biologists in voicing opposition to the use of chemical weapons in war and in propagandizing for United States ratification of the Geneva Protocol of 1925, an international treaty that enjoins signatories from such actions.

By 1969, when tests were revealed indicating that 2,4,5-T contained an impurity that could cause malformation of developing embryos in pregnant female rats, the awful possibility emerged that human embryos might have been so affected. I determined to try to get permission to visit Vietnam during my spring-term sabbatical in 1971 to see for myself the damages wrought by the chemical war and to bring back any available data. Early in 1971 I was informed that I would probably be approved for a visit to North Vietnam as part of a delegation of scientists. But when the arrangements were finally completed, the delegation had dwindled to two men, Dr. Ethan Signer, a virus expert from the Massachusetts Institute of Technology, and myself. We were scheduled to leave in mid-April for a three-week trip, including about one week in North Vietnam.

Then came the electrifying news of the American table-tennis team's entry into China. This event, a signal to the whole world that the People's Republic was prepared to open its doors to the West, was for us a timely coincidence as well. It motivated us to take advantage of the tantalizing proximity of China to North Vietnam by applying for Chinese visas. Having filed the appropriate papers through the Chinese embassy in Ottawa, we departed for Hanoi. We had actually been there for twelve days, had toured exhaustively, and had experienced the honor of an interview with Premier Pham Van Dong and other leaders when we were summoned rather suddenly to the Chinese Embassy. There we were finally notified of the absolutely unexpected granting of our visa requests.

Thus, my Chinese adventure began when Ethan Signer and I entered the People's Republic on May 10, 1971. From the very first, the gracious hospitality of our hosts, the Academy of Sciences, was manifest in the careful arrangements they had made for our stay. Luxurious living accommodations, the finest cuisine, sensitive interpreters, and comfortable transportation enhanced and expedited a memorable introduction to a fascinating land. Our Chinese hosts sought to show us not only the features of their country they considered most important but also many we suggested as of special interest to us.

One of the items on our Chinese visa applications had asked for names of friends in the People's Republic of China. Not knowing the purpose of the question, I had, after much hesitation, written in the names of several Chinese scientists who had been one-time professional colleagues in the United States. The heartwarming result was being met at the train station in Peking by Lee Cheng-li, a former research associate at Yale University and now a professor at the University of Peking, and at the airport in Shanghai by Loo Shih-wei, a former graduate student at Caltech, now a senior plant physiologist at Shanghai's Academy of Sciences. The open, uninterpreted discussions we had with such friends expanded our view of China far beyond the perspective of the guided tour.

Soon after our arrival, we were asked what we would like to see and do. We listed universities, all aspects of city life, communal operation, and of course such tourist "musts" as the Great Wall, Forbidden City, and Ming tombs. All this was crowded in, plus firsthand observation of acupuncture in surgery, visits to trade and industrial exhibits, and evenings of banqueting, operas, and movies. We also mentioned a desire to meet Chairman Mao Tse-tung. At first this request produced great amusement and protestations of unlikelihood among our hosts. A day or so later they told us

Talking about China in English with professional colleagues broadened our perspective for touring. This lively group in Peking includes three who have studied in the United States, from left to right, Prof. Lee Cheng-li, Department of Botany, Peking University and Dr. Tang Pei-sung of the Institute of Botany, Academy of Sciences, Peking, and at the extreme right, Prof. Tsui Cheng, also of the Institute of Botany, Peking.

such a meeting would in fact not be possible but that we would be "pleased by what has been arranged." Shortly thereafter we were chauffeured to Peking's Great Hall of the People for a meeting and more than two hours of conversation with Premier Chou En-lai.

He talked simply, openly, directly. He stated clearly China's nonaggressive attitude in the international scene and her genuine desire for friendship with the United States in spite of disappointment with many of that country's past actions. He spoke with pride of his country's progress and of the specific contributions of socialism. He surprised and delighted us with his knowledge of political and social problems in the United States as well as his interest in us and our scientific work. He then suggested that since we had already conferred with two Heads of State, Premier Pham Van Dong and himself, it would be fitting for us to meet Prince Norodom Sihanouk, whose Cambodian government in exile China supports, and Kuo Mo-jo, president of the Chinese Academy of Sciences, and he subsequently arranged for those two valuable additions to our tour.

The impact of being with this remarkable man colored our every impression of China. His confidence in the growing well-being of his country was borne out in our visits to city and countryside, schools and hospitals. His statement of desire for rapprochement with the United States is now a matter of daily history.

The traditional Chinese farewell bids departing guests to "return soon again" and adds the hope that "your family will come too." The memory of that sentiment expressed when Ethan and I left China in 1971 and the effect of seeing so much, yet not nearly enough, kindled that hope into the reality of a second visit to China in June and July of 1972.

My family did in fact accompany me. Both my wife, Dale, and my daughter, Beth, became intrigued and enthusiastic as

An unexpected highlight of my 1971 trip. Premier Chou En-lai received Ethan Signer (to the right of the Premier) and myself at the Great Hall of the People in Peking. At the far left is P'an Ch'un, our friend and guide, and third from left, Kuo Mo-jo, President of the Academy of Sciences.

we talked about my 1971 trip. Once again the necessary visas were granted, and we were welcomed back. When we landed at the Shanghai airport on June 6, 1972, it was the beginning of a much longer and very different excursion.

As an academic family, we were bound to bring a diversity of special interests and expectations to traveling in China. My wife, a former nursery school teacher and director, now a child psychologist for a community clinic, hoped to observe not only the formal educational process but also techniques for the treatment of unusual or deviant children. My daughter, a potter, was intensely interested in Chinese art forms and especially in the organization of artistic effort and the creative ambience for the individual artist. And as a university professor, I wanted to expand my knowledge of the Chinese educational system—to comprehend more fully the training of Chinese youth for their role in tomorrow's world. To fulfill such high expectations would require much more time for study than our trip allowed, but the attempt to do so left us with a useful grasp of the dramatic restructuring of the quality of life in the New China.

In the course of our travels we repeated much of the sightseeing of my 1971 trip, but extra time allowed more depth to our touring. We concentrated on visits to nurseries, primary and middle schools, public recreational facilities, and craft factories. During the two trips we saw four universities (Chungsan in Canton, Futan in Shanghai, Peking and Tsinghua in Peking) and four research institutes of the Chinese Academy of Sciences (Botanical and Microbiological Institutes in Peking, Plant Physiological and Biochemical Institutes in Shanghai).

Although all of us appreciated the continuing solicitude of Chinese hospitality, we soon realized that the demands of having our every hour tightly scheduled prevented some of the simpler, more spontaneous pleasures to be found in more direct contact with the Chinese themselves. We requested relief from the isolation of always staying in the luxury hotels reserved for foreigners, traveling in limousines, and touring institutions with large committees; for the most part our hosts gladly acceded. Most important, because a one-day visit to the Malu People's Commune in 1971 had indicated that the heart of China resides in the countryside, we re-

[6]

Shih Chen-yu stands in the inner courtyard of his compound at Lugou Ch'iao Commune surrounded by some of his grandchildren. Friendship with this dignified, warmhearted peasant, who opened his home to us in 1972, afforded us a direct understanding and appreciation of daily life in People's China today.

quested a longer visit on a commune. Although I am sure our hosts will never understand our perverse desire for a more informal, open view of their country, they finally did understand its importance to us.

The consequences could hardly have satisfied, or astounded, us more. Our hosts arranged a visit of several weeks at the Marco Polo Bridge People's Commune near Peking. There we lived with Shih Chen-yu, a seventy-three-year-old peasant, his wife, children, and grandchildren. We worked in the wheat fields, rice paddies, and vegetable plots of the production team to which the family belonged. We observed their schools, medical stations, stores, and factories. For us, this unique experience put flesh on the bones of China's publicly stated goals and claims of progress toward them. Moreover, it rewarded us with warm, new friendships and thereby a closer understanding of a foreign culture.

Knowing that China is a closed society, readers may question whether the view we obtained represents the real China. It is easy to imagine that the Chinese would show us only their leading commune, most efficient factory, most modern laboratory, newest apartment houses, and finest stores. As foreigners only slightly familiar with the language, we had to depend for much of our information on interpreters. While I am sure that the Chinese did not take us to see any feature of their society of which they were ashamed and that they put their best foot forward in every possible instance, I am equally sure we could not have been completely misled. Not only were we free to walk around by ourselves in the cities without guides, without interpreters, and, so far as we know, without surveillance, but we were also free to record, almost without restriction, whatever we saw with camera or pen. Moreover, we benefited greatly from the many special circumstances surrounding our visits, especially the unsupervised conversations with Chinese friends, fluent speakers of English, who provided frank answers to many provocative questions Americans ask about China. These permitted us to calibrate our reactions with facts gleaned from more official sources. Having applied reasonable mental checks and balances, I feel confident that our impressions reflect an accurate picture of society in China today.

[8]

Sharing them is the important next step, taken in the hope of contributing to a bank of knowledge about China—lack of which has too long prevented the understanding between our two countries that could draw us together in friendship.

A very young citizen of the People's Republic of China extended a most cheerful greeting to visiting Americans.

2

A New Look at an Old Country

AT THE AIRPORT in Hanoi, Ethan Signer and I were the only travelers, ours was the only plane; there were no taxis, no luggage or porters, no noise, or press, or confusion. The mood was austere, completely in keeping with the low priority for travel of a nation at war. We felt excitement and not a little apprehension as we looked forward in May 1971 to visiting China, a country that few Americans and no American scientists had entered for twenty-two years.

The flight from Hanoi to Nanning, South China, longtime center for trade with North Vietnam, takes about one and a half hours. We made it in a Soviet Ilyushin twin-propeller-engine transport, converted for use by the Civil Aviation Administration of China (CAAC). The small, scrupulously clean, gleaming white airplane was embellished with a tribute to Mao's thought in gigantic red-painted Chinese characters. Our companion on the trip was a representative of Hanoi's Committee for Solidarity with the American People. When we landed at about 8:00 P.M., there, smiling up at us from the bottom of the boarding steps, was the Chinese government's official welcoming delegation, all dressed alike in classic Mao-style tunics, with bright red Mao buttons on their breasts. There were two local officials and two men who had journeyed all the way from Peking that morning expressly to meet us, guide us, and accompany us during our entire stay in China. One, introduced as our interpreter, was Liu Tze-han, a slender, bespectacled, thirty-one-year-old linguist, and the other, P'an Ch'un, a husky fifty-five-year-old, was chairman of the Revolutionary Committee at the Botanical Research Institute in Peking.

When we were introduced to P'an, I thought I had misunderstood his title. Revolutionary Committee at a botanical research institute? There must be something wrong with the translation. But it was absolutely accurate, for, as we soon discovered, every institution in China—commune, factory, municipality, university research institute—is supervised by a group called a Revolutionary Committee (RC).

Our new friend, P'an Ch'un, was thus the first of the many political administrators we encountered during our stay in China, and a most agreeable first specimen he was. The sinister implications evoked by the realities of Revolutionary Committee surveillance were completely dispelled by his smiling, hearty presence. Efficient, cheerful, sensitive, he made getting around in China pleasant in every imaginable way.

After introductions and handshaking all around on the airport runway, we adjourned to the terminal building, where a ceremonial hot washcloth and tea were provided for us before we were taken into a private dining room for a gala meal. There were four delicious main dishes (fowl, fish, meat, and vegetables) and mounds of steamed rice, then soup, and finally pineapple and mandarin orange segments, cake, and tea. The food was accompanied by three different alcoholic beverages: cold lager-type beer, a sweet grape wine, and a fiery sorghum liquor named *mao-tai*. All were agreeable, and Chinese hospitality induced a temptation to excess. The conversation consisted chiefly of the amenities and many toasts. We learned to say *yoidi yi* (friendship first) and *kambei* (bottoms up). It left us sated, limp, and pliable. I could not help wondering if changing planes were always like this in China.

Then it appeared that we had a decision to make before proceeding. It was possible to fly directly from Nanning to Peking or to go first to Kwangchou. So ignorant were Ethan and I that we failed to recognize Kwangchou as the alternate designation of Canton, where, at that time, China's International Trade Fair was in progress. When we told our hosts that we would prefer to go directly to Peking, they looked a little surprised but said nothing; they simply poured us another cup of tea and kept the conversation going. By imperceptible degrees, we became aware how much more advantageous it would be for us to go to Kwangchou first and eventually took that option. This was an unusual example of gentle Chinese persuasiveness. I don't remember being told to change my mind or even urged to do so, but an atmosphere was created in which we did in fact change our minds, and we were later quite content that we had.

With this matter settled, we left the banquet room and proceeded immediately to the runway, where another plane, again bright white and bedecked with huge red Chinese characters extolling Mao, stood waiting for us. We thought at first that it was a private plane just for us, but once we had been seated with P'an and Liu at our sides, other passengers were allowed to board. They had been waiting all the hours it took for our hosts to receive us with appropriate hospitality. It was suddenly all too evident that they had not enjoyed the leisurely rest and a sumptuous meal like ours, and we were quite embarrassed by such conspicuously special treatment. We were to experience this feeling many times before our trip to China was over. It is a basic attribute of good Chinese manners to spare nothing to make guests very, very comfortable.

Taking off in a Chinese plane is very much like taking off in an American plane; the passengers are all strangers; a lighted sign commands that seat belts be fastened and cigarettes extinguished, and magazines or chewing gum are distributed by a typically confidence-inspiring stewardess. On our twenty-five-passenger plane, she was husky, cheerful, round-faced; she wore loose-fitting, dark blue trousers and a square-cut white blouse hanging outside the pants. Her hair was also square-cut, in what we used to call a Buster Brown hairdo, and her face was continually wreathed in smiles. No sooner had the pilot leveled off at flying altitude and turned off the seat belt sign, than she served us all some orange juice. She was exceedingly conscientious as to the comfort of all her passengers, albeit somewhat unorthodox by our standards. Standing in the center aisle, she made an announcement. I asked Liu, our interpreter, what she had said. "She is going to sing some

songs for us," he said, and to our great surprise, she burst into song with great gusto. Several passengers immediately joined in. I looked over at P'an, who mouthed some of the words, smiled at us, and sang softly. The first song was entitled "Good Health to Chairman Mao," and when the stewardess finished singing it, she was accorded a vigorous round of applause. Pleased, she carried on with a still more sprightly number, and everyone sang enthusiastically and clapped hands in rhythm. This second song was called "Let's All Get Together" and was a harvest song popular with the peasants. By the time our plane landed in Kwangchou, a little over three hundred miles from Nanning, our community of strangers had been knit into a friendly group by virtue of singing together. What a refreshing difference from the earphones and eight-track music selectors offered on the huge American air transports!

Again, in Canton, we were greeted formally by a reception committee of civic leaders and representatives of the Municipal Revolutionary Committee. The leader of the group was Li Ming-koo, head of the Scientific and Technical Division of Kwangtung Province and a veteran of the famous Long March of the Red Chinese Army in 1935, from the South to the Northwest of China, a trek that ended in the consolidation of the leadership and power of the Communists. The genial, outgoing nature of this tall and handsome man infected this greeting ceremony with great warmth and camaraderie. He invited us to take drinks and tea at the terminal building. To get there we walked along a path lined rather awesomely with twenty-five-foot-high billboards. Here in gold and white lettering on red backgrounds, in English as well as Chinese, the redundant messages are pounded home: "Unite and fight to defeat U.S. aggressors and all their running dogs," "Down with revisionism" and "Dare to Think, Dare to Act." Dominating all, inside and outside the terminal, were huge poster pictures of Mao Tse-tung, Marx, Engels, Lenin, and Stalin. We felt genuinely intimidated by the omnipresence of the exhortations. Not till near the end of our trip could we begin to escape their impact.

The terminal building itself is a good-looking, modern construction of vast proportions, hardly necessary for the twenty-five or thirty of us who were the only passengers in evidence. One

[14]

The rather awesome entrance of the Tung Fang Hotel in Canton belies the hospitality and comfort within.

wall, all glass, looks out on the landing field, so expansive that the two or three planes were almost lost. Obviously built to handle the much heavier air traffic of the future, it is all the more impressive for the lack of hubbub and litter usually found in such buildings.

Canton, with a population of about two million (population

figures are always indefinite because there has been no official census since 1953), is China's seventh largest city. Although they share the written language and cultural traditions of the dominant (95 percent) Sino-Tibetan or Han Chinese, the Cantonese speak a dialect unintelligible to speakers of Mandarin, the dialect of the vast majority of the population. Looking forward to visiting an industrialized urban center did not prepare us for the palm trees of a subtropical setting, the cleanliness, and quiet streets we encountered as we were driven from the airport to the Tung Fang (East Wind) Hotel. In this atmosphere, the once again well-designed, modern building looked especially stunning, though the entrance was flanked by two very strongly worded exhortations: "Unite and Fight U.S. Imperialism" and "Support the heroic peoples of Indochina in their fight against U.S. aggression." These sentiments had no carryover into hospitality, however, as each of us was ushered into a private suite of sitting room, bedroom, and bathroom. For visiting Americans, life in the proletarian Communist world of the New China is not exactly spartan.

Our first full day in China started at 7:30 with breakfast American style in the dining room of a hotel that, like all busy international hotels, was simply bursting with businessmen from all the countries of the world—all, that is, except the United States

This impressive building houses Canton's International Trade Fair, a semi-annual event where businessmen from all over the world can see and buy the latest Chinese agricultural and industrial products.

Chairman Mao emphasizes continuously that China's well-being depends primarily on agricultural productivity. That this notion inspires the peasants is admirably depicted in the huge poster that dominates the hall of agriculture at Canton's International Trade Fair.

and Russia. There were no Chinese guests. Dominated by the Japanese, who occupied an entire guest house of their own, these visitors were in Canton for the Trade Fair, in hopes of promoting Chinese trade with their various nations.

Like all other spectacles in China, the Trade Fair (held for one month, semiannually since 1957) is meant to impress as well as to educate. The main exposition building and the two smaller ones some distance away were gay with banners and the ubiquitous political slogans against the parklike setting of paths, trees, and formal plantings. Exhibits included working models, photo displays, and samples of products. Off the main exhibit halls were small tearooms, where foreign businessmen could consummate agreements. The entire operation seemed to be efficiently run, and we got the impression that much business was actually being transacted.

We chose to visit the halls for agriculture, light industry, clothing and textiles, and fish. This was a small selection of the total number of exhibit halls, which would have taken many days to see. The agriculture hall is presided over by a great color portrait of Chairman Mao talking to smiling peasants in the midst of a grain field ready for harvest. Samples of buckwheat, millet, beans

[17]

of various kinds, soybeans, oats, castor bean, corn, wheat, and rice were all displayed. According to one Mao slogan, "Agriculture is the foundation, and industry is the guiding factor." Another, "In agriculture, learn from Tachai," referred to an especially heroic, and partly successful, effort to create terraces of soil out of bare rock at a commune bearing that name. Clearly, the 80 percent of the Chinese people who live in the countryside, mainly on communes, are considered the foundation of the Chinese economy, and among their endeavors, grain production is emphasized above all: rice in the south, wheat further north, and millet in the far north. The main agricultural exports are rice and meats.

Also featured in the agricultural pavilion were booths with photographs and literature extolling the efforts of pioneers in reforestation, reclamation of wasteland (especially in the Gobi Desert), and a tide-harnessing project. It all pointed to self-reliance as the basis and heroic self-abnegating labor as the touchstone of progress—and it was somehow reminiscent of an earlier day in America.

The light-industry pavilion also promulgated self-help with the slogan, "Learn from Taching," the industrial model equivalent to Tachai for agriculture. In all industry, utilization of every possible by-product is emphasized. For example, one chemical-works exhibit demonstrated the use of sugar cane to produce not only sugar but ethyl alcohol, pulp, and paper as well. In addition, former waste pulp was being used to grow yeast for feeding to livestock and, after chemical breakdown, for spraying on crops to increase their yield.

Approaching the clothing and textile pavilion with our stereotype of the dun-colored baggy trousers and jackets seen everywhere in China, we were surprised at the diversity in color and style of the apparel shown. Cotton was the chief fabric used (as befits the world's largest producer of cotton cloth), but silk, wool, and synthetics were also represented. None of the garments would achieve distinction as Western-world haute couture, but they were certainly of good quality and esthetically put together. The foreign buyers seemed interested and the prices even lower than might be expected, presumably to meet the competition of inexpensive Japanese goods.

[18]

*The Shanghai Industrial Exhibit is a permanent display featuring
current models of machinery manufactured in China.*

We began to learn the Chinese monetary system. The basic
denomination is the *yuan,* 100 *fen,* or Chinese cents. 2.37 yuan
equal $1.00, but there is no equivalency in terms of purchasing
power: 18 fen ($.075) buys a pound of rice; 5 fen ($.02), a
bus ride; 150 yuan ($60), a bicycle; 3 to 5 yuan ($1.20 to
$1.60) a month, apartment rent plus utilities. Obviously not only
the exchange rate but the variance in price structure must be kept
in mind in noting costs in China.

If the Canton Trade Fair is representative of the industrial
output of the people of China, then it must be said that the country, though not industrialized in the Western sense, is definitely not
unindustrialized. Rather it is underindustrialized, for the Chinese
clearly have the know-how and capacity for industrial expansion,
when, as, and if they decide it would be advantageous. They
are self-sufficient in the production of petroleum and other energy
sources. They have learned to produce massive electric generators,

drill presses, trucks, tractors, combines, passenger vehicles of all kinds, precision tools, medical instruments, electronic devices, chemicals, foam rubber, and semiconductors. This has been accomplished without losing sight of such traditional skills as ivory and jade carving, painting, embroidery, making lacquer ware, wood carving, and cloisonné, which also were displayed.

The fair was more impressive in another sense. There was absolutely no advertising, no hint of competition, no commercialism —only the major lesson, that China has stabilized and is capable of mobilizing its resources and its population to produce all the various commodities characteristic of the modern world. It offers the world a gigantic potential market, a massive producer, and an opportunity for peaceful intercourse. No foreign traveler could fail to grasp this message. And for us, visitors of one day, with such different expectations, the effect was shocking.

As we were leaving the exhibition halls, a sudden burst of shouting by a noisy group cascading down a stairway shattered the formal, almost studious quiet of the fair. When we expressed our surprise to our guides, they explained, laughingly, that the world's Ping-Pong champions were making a triumphal tour of the Trade Fair and were being pursued by excited fans trying to get Ping-Pong paddles autographed by their heroes. Hero worship, at least, is the same the world over. Our interest led to quick arrangements for a meeting. The champions had been spirited away from the crowd into a small rest area, but they graciously consented to share their bit of rest time with us, so we passed through the barrier, were introduced, and quickly shook hands with both the male and the female members of the group. None spoke English, but through the interpreters they conveyed their surprise and genuine pleasure to learn that we were Americans. The crowd looked on with great interest and envy, but we heard and saw no sign of disapproval that we were being given special treatment.

Our visit to the fair concluded with the inevitable cup of tea and refreshments in the company of the officials who had been our guides. They asked us, most sincerely, for our impressions of the fair. They said they would be pleased to receive our criticisms so that they could improve their performance in the future. As it was the third time we had been asked for criticisms since entering

中华人民共和国政府声明

全力支援印度支那三国人民的抗美救国战争
GIVE ALL-OUT SUPPORT AND ASSISTANCE TO THE THREE PEOPLES OF INDOCHINA IN THEIR WAR AGAINST U S AGGRESSION AND FOR NATIONAL SALVATION

Two rarities in Shanghai: the hostility of this military poster and the use of motorized vehicles. This automobile is a recent Shanghai-built model.

China (we had received similar requests at the Nanning airport and the Tung Fang Hotel), we began to understand the comprehensiveness of this policy. And so it evolved in every institution we observed. No matter how inexpert we were in the area, and no matter how cursory our view of the operation, we were solemnly asked to contribute to improvement by giving criticism. At first we demurred, saying that we really didn't know much about the operation in question and that we were sure they were doing the best possible job under the circumstances. They were always disappointed with such a remark, however, and genuinely seemed to desire constructive comments. Subsequently, we tried to note one or two shortcomings in order to be prepared for the discussion session, and our hosts seemed much happier with this practice. I don't know the true outcome of our efforts, but it was obvious that, as appreciative guests, we were expected to play our roles in this little ceremony, and we determined not to fall short.

[21]

Sightseeing that first afternoon was somewhat frustrating and acquainted us with the kind of difficulties to anticipate in touring China. Our guides conducted us in shiny black, Russian-made Volga limousines with dark curtains across the back windows that shielded us from scrutiny but also prevented easy observation of the world outside. Moreover, their conversation tended to pedantic instruction about what we were going to see rather than what we were passing. As the entire welcoming committee accompanied us, we formed a veritable caravan of Volgas honking its way past miles and miles of fascinating streets. The paved, tree-lined blocks abounded with people: on foot, on bicycles, in stores, in windows and doorways of apartments, engaged in the countless, day-to-day activities that comprise life. But our drivers, bent on their destination, avoided all that intriguing humanity and took us instead to a quiet, almost lonely park, "The Mausoleum of the Canton Commune." It commemorates an uprising on December 13, 1927, in which four thousand revolutionaries were slain.

We could understand why they took us there, for the park is indeed stunning, both as to its landscaping and its memorial buildings. Especially outstanding, the Soviet-Chinese friendship pavilion commemorates the aid given to China by the U.S.S.R. Despite

The formal beauty in Canton's Park of the Martyrs typifies the care given to the many public parks in all of China's cities.

Near the Park of the Martyrs in Canton we saw the pleasant entrance of a small district hospital.

currently poor relations between the two great powers, no attempt has been made to remove the building or to change its name. The Korean pavilion honors one hundred and fifty volunteers from that country who fought and died with the Chinese during the war against Japan. A pathway through the park leads to a series of magnificent vistas, created by formal plantings artfully placed so as to create one striking scene after another. As we passed one of the entrances, our guides called our special attention to the Kwangchou Hospital just across the street.

The park is admirably maintained, partly by student labor. Entire class groups contribute one-half day per week to plant, prune, weed, build roads and trails, or otherwise improve the park. We saw one such student group raking, shoveling, and clearing litter. They seemed to be enjoying it and smiled and waved as we approached.

Nearby we went, first by elevator, then by stairs, to the top of

Canton's highest building—the fourteenth story of the People's Mansion Guest House—from which rooftop we enjoyed a panoramic view over the city and received our first, and almost only, injunction not to take pictures. We learned that we were free to photograph almost anything on the ground without requesting permission, but from a height or in an airplane, never. The only places on the ground that were barred to us were airports and major street intersections in some cities. From our vantage we could see the sections of Canton ceded to various European nations following the Opium Wars of 1839–42, where foreigners were allowed to live and work outside Chinese legal jurisdiction. The Germans had actually built the first part of the People's Mansion; it was not completed until 1965. We began to sense a basis for the intense nationalist feeling involved in the ousting of foreign influences from China and the residual resentment against the "foreign devils" who had exploited the people and forced opium and other degradations upon the country. Now we could view playgrounds where children were playing basketball and practicing gymnastics and whole neighborhoods of new apartment houses and factory buildings. For the most part, however, the scene was indeed that of a large industrialized city anywhere, gray and monotonous, but with few high buildings, only a hint of smog, few automobiles, little city roar.

Later in the day, at our request, our guides took us back into the busy part of the city. We stopped along the Pearl River, about five hundred yards wide at this point, the banks crowded by commercial streets and walks, obviously a favorite gathering place for Canton citizens. In the past, it had been cluttered with scows and junks on which otherwise homeless people lived. Today the People's Republic of China boasts that it has given all such people permanent places to live, and neat apartment houses were pointed out to us as examples of such residences. The river, spanned by an attractive new bridge, seemed clean, orderly, and free of pollution, its traffic of junks and barges employed only in commercial shipping.

If we thought our crowded day might occasion a letup in our social schedule for the evening, we were greatly mistaken. There was to be a banquet hosted by Li Ming-koo, and for it we were driven to a magnificent guest house, obviously a showplace for

Many stone Buddhas like the one above (left) are carved into the walls of a canyon near Hangchou. At the Lung Fa Botanical Gardens are grown hundreds of species of plants to be transplanted in parks and streets everywhere in the Peking Municipality. This charming dwarf pine (right) is 200 years old.

foreign dignitaries. We entered through large, intricately carved stone gates onto a drive of a quarter mile through a dense, lush, tropical garden. The mansion itself sprawled low into this setting with wide overhanging roofs, reminiscent of Frank Lloyd Wright's designs. The interior, like so many in China, leaned to European overstuffed ornateness, which surprised us, since we had anticipated more of a Japanese spareness. The party included not only the official members of our reception committee, but also several members of scholarly and scientific institutions in the Canton region. Again Chinese hospitality was overpowering but certainly enlivened that evening by Li Ming-koo's amiability and humanity. He offered toast after toast with *mao-tai* to amity and friendship between our two peoples. One could not refuse to *kambei* for such an important cause, but the result of all the food and drink was a resolution to pace ourselves for the long haul ahead if we were to survive several weeks in China. It was also becoming madly frustrating to speak solely in social amenities,

[25]

especially with such a man as Li, intelligent, witty, fun-loving, exuding an air of competence and sophistication.

Following dinner we were taken to a movie of the ballet, "The Red Detachment of Women," one of nine Revolutionary Exemplary Works—dramas, operas, and ballets that are shown continually in China. We appreciated the opportunity to mingle with the Cantonese in a favorite recreation but were more than a little disturbed to realize the very real sterility of their entertainment opportunities. The melodramatic plot, extraordinarily naive by American standards, involved highly stylized heroes (the Red Army and their women allies), villains (the Kuomintang, landlords, thieves), and the heroics of the good guys finally overcoming the machinations of the bad. Perhaps it seemed less trite to the Chinese because the realities are still very close. When we rose to

The approach to the Ming Tombs near Peking is guarded by many imposing stone warriors, about 12 feet high. Mythical animals, too, guard these treasure troves of the fourteenth to seventeenth centuries only recently reopened to the citizens of the People's Republic.

leave, everyone most solicitously made way for the honored guests.

The rest of our brief stay in Canton continued to preview what we might expect as travelers in the New China. For example, on the last day we were instructed to leave our packed bags in the hallway of the hotel before we departed for the morning's tour of Chungsan University. We realized suddenly that confidence in the honesty of those responsible for personal possessions is a commonplace in China. Nothing is stolen, certainly not from foreigners, and no tips or special arrangements are necessary to accomplish this. Nor were we ever cautioned about any sort of danger in city streets. Since reports of pre-Revolutionary China had always emphasized the prevalence of thievery and thuggery in most cities, we could only marvel at how this nation has managed to achieve such effective law and order in the years since 1949.

En route to the university we traversed a stretch of blocks with old-style colonnades extending over the sidewalks, a graceful accommodation to the pleasures of shade in this semitropical clime. The first floors of these buildings generally housed stores where people were window-shopping, strolling leisurely, or proceeding briskly on more urgent affairs. We noticed many women and some men wearing red armbands and were told that they were marshals "to help maintain civil order." Whatever their means of maintaining order, it did not involve the obvious use of force, since they possessed no weapons of any sort and did not appear to be especially burly or otherwise threatening.

Chungsan was the first of several universities I was to visit during my trips to China, and the pattern set at this institution in Canton could serve as a model for every other such visit.

Upon our arrival on the campus, we were received by the Revolutionary Committee, lined up in front of a central building, applauding vigorously. This procedure was followed in every classroom and laboratory of every institution we visited, and we quickly learned that it was appropriate for us to applaud our hosts as well. (Such a salutation, so unnatural to Americans, is actually the warmest and most respectful of Chinese welcomes.) We then entered a comfortable lounge and were introduced to the various members of the group, who proceeded to tell us about their university. Here is what we learned:

[27]

Chungsan University, formerly known as Kwangchou University, was founded in 1924 by Sun Yat-sen on the site of the old missionary-founded Lingnan University. In 1925, when Sun died, the name was changed to honor him, Chungsan being a way of saying his name. In 1966 the university was completely reorganized as the result of the Cultural Revolution. Before that time, the university did not have much impact on society—"it followed the reactionary line of Liu Shao-ch'i (Head of State until 1966) and his agents." During the Cultural Revolution, Chungsan, like all Chinese universities, was closed, and when it reopened in 1970, its administration was placed in the hands of a Revolutionary Committee of twenty members. Finally the structure of the ubiquitous RC was made clear to us. An RC always includes representation from three groups of people: the workers, or masses, who compose the organization in question (at Chungsan this meant students and faculty); political cadres (like our friend and guide, P'an Ch'un), well versed in Marxism, Leninism, Maoism, and adept at learning organizational details of the institutions they are trained to manage; and finally, the People's Liberation Army (PLA), Chairman Mao's chief support in reasserting the power of the central government during the most violent and troublesome phases of the Cultural Revolution, whose presence on all RCs guarantees a determinative role for the central government.

The visit to Chungsan resulted more in an accumulation of statistics like these than in an informal experience of everyday university operations. The Chinese seem to delight in such crisp, precise presentations. If, as our hosts at Chungsan claimed, enrollments are increasing and admissions are drawn from a far wider base, they have just cause for the pride they feel in their university.

At Chungsan, as everywhere, we were the focus of prolonged staring. The students seemed friendly and courteous, yet walking among clusters of strangers who stared unrelentingly at one's person was rather uncomfortable. Of course, the sheer physical differences they perceived in our larger stature, longer noses and hair, lighter eyes, more sauntering gait, and Western clothes must have been fascinating. But surely some residual feelings about foreign devils lay behind the stares. And surely some early conditioning about sinister Orientals contributed to our uneasiness.

[28]

Our farewell to Canton was a luncheon given for us by Pu Chih-lung and his wife, Lee Tsui-ying, both 1946 Ph.D.s from the University of Minnesota, now insect physiologists at Chungsan. Included in the party were other Chinese fluent in English. The resultant conversations without the intervention of an interpreter not only speeded up the give and take but permitted us to ask questions frankly and get unambiguous answers. It was a warm act of hospitality; Lee Tsui-ying cooked a simple but elegant meal, and the glimpse of their spacious, comfortable, modern apartment was a rare treat.

Then we were off once more with Liu and P'an to Canton's airport for the flight to Peking. Although the weather seemed fine in Canton, we were informed that there would be storms en route. We took off, but when we were within an hour of completing the 1,428 miles to Peking from Canton, the pilot announced that because of an intense thunderstorm we were going to set down in Chengchou, capital of Honan Province, and Liu and P'an told us why. Lacking jets, and determined to maintain air safety, Chinese aviation authorities absolutely forbid air travel during storms. This procedure, of course, is bound to change, as even now the

Unlike China's airports, railway stations teem with activity. Here at Yanzhou, en route from Shanghai to Peking, even the youngest traveler helps with luggage.

Chinese are acquiring jet transports, capable of flying above such weather.

We spent about two hours in Chengchou's airport waiting for the weather to clear, during which time we wandered about to observe what we could of the countryside. Suddenly the sky was filled with a cluster of old World War I-type biplanes disgorging clouds of parachutes from several thousand feet above the airfield. We assumed it was a military training operation, as there must have been two dozen planes involved. The parachutists landed and boarded lorries, which then brought them to the terminal building. Imagine our surprise on discovering that some of them were young women! Liu explained to us that this was part of the usual paramilitary training given to workers from factories and communes on a volunteer basis as part of a national fitness and preparedness program.

Finally the word came that the weather was so bad our plane was grounded for the night. P'an and Liu then decided that we would save time by taking a train scheduled to leave at 10:30 that evening and to arrive the next morning in Peking. For the interim, we would stay in a local guest house patronized by many Chinese in transit. This was an interesting experience because it

Travelers can wash up and buy refreshments quickly right on the platform of a brief stop between Shanghai and Peking.

Peking's central Railroad Station is an agreeable place to arrive.

permitted us to evaluate accommodations that had not been prepared for us in advance and that were typical of all smallish cities.

The guest house was satisfactory in every way. Smaller than the
hotels we had seen in Canton but, if anything, more attractive and
modern, it was set in parklike environs along a tree-lined road
adjacent to meticulously manicured fields of grain. We bathed and
rested in our rooms and, after a fine meal, took off for the railroad
station.

The train itself was a wonderful surprise and worthy of emulation by American railroads. Not only did it run exactly on time, but—even more impressive—the sleeping compartments were comfortable and spotlessly clean, the attendants overwhelmingly gracious and courteous, and the food about as good as we could have eaten in a fine restaurant. Adjacent to our compartment was a clean washroom. The only challenge was a one-hole squat toilet, which took a bit of adjustment for our Western bodies.

At 6:15 in the morning we were aroused by the strains of "The East Is Red," piped throughout the train and followed by news on the loudspeaker. At 7:00 we were joined by Liu and P'an for a discussion of travel plans. Breakfast was at 7:30 and included three eggs with Canadian-type bacon, toast and butter, and warm sweet milk—shades of childhood!

At the Peking station another large welcoming delegation awaited us. New names, old routine, except for my friend, Lee Cheng-li, now a professor at the University of Peking. Once again our baggage appeared as if by magic. Then we were whisked away in shiny black Shanghai limousines and settled in comfort at the Hsin Ch'iao Hotel, where we spent the next several days of our first fifteen in China.

Our impressions at this moment were certainly mixed. Clearly, the Chinese were capable of, and addicted to, efficient and gracious hospitality. Our hotel rooms, food, and receptions were going to be not only polite and correct, but even lavish; we would be conducted on tours of every kind of institution in China, and information about them would be poured upon us; our transport from place to place would be expeditiously arranged; and nothing would be spared to give us the greatest comfort possible, even though arranging all such convenience was often difficult. Such careful planning, however, implied as well the disruption caused by our traveling in speedy, honking limousines, the isolation in hotels exclusively for foreigners, the constant accompaniment of the numerous members of RCs, even eating only Western food unless we specifically requested *jungwo fan* (local cuisine). Did these arrangements stem solely from the dictates of Chinese hospitality, or did our hosts intend to prevent more direct contact with the people? We did not know, but the routine never varied. Equally discomfiting was the knowledge that no urban Chinese enjoyed

Our room at the Hop'ing Hotel in Shanghai overlooked a main street on the waterfront. Modern barges and ancient junks work side by side in the harbor. A traffic policeman directs the flow of buses, pedestrians, push-carts, and bicycles from an elevated control post.

a life so luxurious as ours. What is more, we had seen nothing of the vast preponderance of the Chinese, the rural population. Nonetheless, the whirlwind tour continued—and continued to engage and absorb us in spite of our doubts. It encompassed the many historical and cultural treasures of Peking, included memorable conversations with Chou En-lai and other leaders, and ended with several days in Shanghai.

Here, two events occurred that illuminated the China we had been missing. During a brief respite in the touring we had a short walk in the streets near our Shanghai hotel. A crowd of young people, curious about our appearance and clothing, our language and identity, started following us. They pressed in around us, actually preventing our progress, and for a moment we experienced panic. Just then, one of the youngest ran up to me and put something into my hand. It was his bright red Mao button, taken from his own shirt and offered smilingly. At this signal, all the youngsters plucked off their buttons and showered them on us. We told our interpreter, Liu, to ask them to stop; we already had enough buttons, and, besides, we were embarrassed because we had nothing to offer them in return. When Liu relayed these words to them, one young man answered in a loud voice while the others all nodded their concurrence. Liu translated: "You have brought us the gift of friendship and that is the most valuable of all."

The second event was a visit to the Malu People's Commune, a glimpse unfortunately of only a few hours—long enough, however, to convince me that in observing communal life lay the opportunity for the most telling examination of the strength and mentality of the New China.

The peasants of labor-rich Malu People's Commune near Shanghai harvest their barley crop with sickle and scythe.

3

Revolution in the Countryside

ABOUT 80 PERCENT of the almost 800 million people of China live and work in the countryside, chiefly on its sixty thousand communes. The generally successful operation of the communes and the nationwide economic plan that directs their activities has converted China from a land of chronic food shortage and frequent starvation to a land that can feed all its people with little or no outside help. No longer is a drought an occasion for panic and widespread starvation, and no longer is the destruction of a flood compounded by hunger and disease. Unlike the Soviet collective farms, which, even after fifty years of experience, still rarely live up to projected agricultural productivity, the Chinese communes prospered instantly. "Why the difference?" is the inevitable question. It was answered for me in part by a brief visit in 1971 to the Malu People's Commune near Shanghai which provided an explanation of the general background and organization of these enterprises. In 1972, a much longer visit at the Marco Polo Bridge People's Commune outside Peking brought deeper understanding of decentralized decision-making, the system of personal incentives, and the high morale central to the progress of these remarkable communities.

The initial shock upon visiting Malu was its size. Almost six thousand acres are farmed—95 percent for rice and cotton, the remainder largely for barley and rape (a herb grown as a forage crop and for its seeds, which are used to make cooking oil). The favorable climate and soil conditions in the wide Yangtze River plain enable the production of two or three crops a year, the output of an active labor force of more than 16,600. This force is supplied by a population of 27,500—more than 6,000 households. For living and working, the total population is divided into fourteen smaller units, brigades, each of which is further divided into ten production teams of about fifty families, or 200 people, including about 120 able-bodied workers.

Efficient administration of an operation that involves 27,500 people demands a tight organization. Realizing this—and the inherent difficulties of achieving it in an undeveloped rural community—prompted my first question, "How do you do it?" My hosts eagerly described their operation. At Malu, as on all communes (and in all factories, municipalities, educational and other institutions), all organizational responsibility lies in the hands of the Revolutionary Committees. Formation of these groups came at the end of the Cultural Revolution—a direct response to Mao's directive for a "three-in-one" leadership combination to carry out the task of struggle-criticism-transformation. The RCs bring together elected representatives of the working masses, members of the People's Liberation Army, and political cadres. RC organization provides at once direct participation of the people in local planning and a link in the chain of command with the next higher authority, the RC of the region, and ultimately the central government.

Planning for the commune originates in a regional master plan, which in turn emanates from the projections encompassing the agricultural needs of the nation as a whole. Sitting at the apex of the communal pyramid of authority, the commune RC determines the overall production program and output goals on the basis of the regional plan; it then allocates quotas to each brigade. The brigade RCs divide these quotas among the production units in their jurisdiction. Functioning as the basic work unit of the structure, each production unit thus starts out each year with a clearly defined task.

How to meet this goal—how many *mus* (1 *mu* = ⅙ acre) of which crop to plant at what season, what the individual responsibilities

Irrigation ditches crisscross the Malu People's Commune, part of China's tremendous effort for water conservation.

are in the planting, irrigation, cultivation, and harvesting of each plot, how rotation will be planned—all ways and means are decided by the production units themselves. They must decide shrewdly and farsightedly, and the individual members must implement their decisions vigorously, for the returns they receive depend on the quality of their work as well as total output. At the end of the year, total crop income is distributed. The government receives about 4 percent for support of its own operations; the commune about ½ percent for administrative costs, 35 percent for production costs, and 10 percent for capital; and the workers about 50 percent, or what is left after all expenses have been covered. Shares are distributed through the brigades for final division by the production units.

In the historical perspective of continuing revolution, China is now moving through the socialist stage. This is the long transitional phase between the "new democratic" stage, the antifeudalist, antiimperialist revolution started by Sun Yat-sen in 1911 that ended in 1949, and the ultimate goal of communism. Politically, the socialist phase is characterized by the transference of leadership from the bourgeoisie to the working classes and economically by the principle, "From each according to his ability, to each according to his work." Translating this guideline into everyday communal practice has brought about the use of a work-point system for estimating rewards based on a standard workday's share in the unit's portion of the distribution.

Within the production units, each worker is evaluated against the standard workday on the basis of attitude, skill, and labor intensity. This involves a town-meeting type of conference, at which the performance of a person or group with typical achievement is established as the norm, and all others are graded above and below accordingly. These evaluations are carried out at various intervals, once a month or once each half year, depending on the planning of the production teams themselves. If a person fails to agree with a grade assigned to him, his close colleagues can usually convince him of its justice and show him where he has fallen down, whereupon he starts to improve. If he is still not persuaded and wants to appeal the decision of the production team, he can approach the Revolutionary Committee of the brigade or even the district. Our informants laughingly added, however, that some such cases had occurred prior to the Cultural Revolution but none since.

Following this system, if a production team as a whole turns in a poor performance, its income will be reduced, and any individual who malingers or does not work to capacity will be downgraded by those working right beside him. The system insures efficient production because it furnishes each worker with a double

High agricultural yields like this rich barley field at Malu have become a reality since communal organization in China.

incentive, as a member of the group and as an individual. This appeal generates very high morale.

Peasant satisfaction is further enhanced because the Revolutionary Committees are elected by reasonably democratic methods. Even though the Communist Party, and particularly the Municipal Revolutionary Committee, have the ultimate power over all enterprises within the region, each individual exerts some measure of personal influence through regular election procedures. Peasants vote in elections for the RC of their brigade and commune (and themselves serve in the decision-making of their own production unit). First, possible candidates are discussed at mass meetings, and nominations are made, always in the light of insuring proper representation from the masses, cadres, and the PLA; from among men and women; and from among young, middle-aged, and old workers. Then secret ballot elections are held, and the candidates with the greatest number of votes are declared elected. The desired end effect is a Revolutionary Committee of responsible persons that can be respected by all. We learned that persons elected to the various RCs can be removed by a superior body, such as the Municipal RC, for reasons of political inadequacy or weakness of character, determined in ways we never fully understood. Despite this, everyone we talked to expressed confidence that the Revolutionary Committees represent the best possible leadership for their organizations.

At Malu the RC of the commune consists of twenty-five members; thirteen represent the working masses; two come from the PLA; and ten are political cadres. Six women and nineteen men make up the committee, evidence of the conscious effort toward a broad base of representation; just a short time ago there were only two. The peasants at Malu spoke of this advance as only a beginning; they acknowledged that women's representation in the RCs still falls far short of their approximately 60-percent representation in the commune's working force. In spite of a national goal of complete equality of the sexes, women do not always receive equal pay for equal work. We heard of one instance of a discrepancy of four work points between the best woman (eight points) and the best man (twelve) on the same job. Furthermore, women are often barred from the jobs of highest pay and greatest responsibility. In the fields the men operate the plows, winnows, and horse carts, while the women are relegated to hand-picking, hoeing, and shoveling grain. Such practice derives in part from physiological differences in size and strength. Our hosts assured us, moreover, that such inequalities have been eliminated on some communes, and they have every expectation that Malu will follow suit. On considering Chinese women's rapid strides toward liberation generally, such progress does seem probable.

The chairman of the RC at Malu, as on most communes, is a political cadre. If the cadre chairman lacks detailed working knowledge of the enterprise, he may entrust the vice-chairman with day-to-day management, while he confines himself to guiding policy according to firmly Maoist directives. He thus oversees continuing political education and strives to simplify administrative affairs and maintain unity of leadership. The Malu chairman, a trusted longtime leader, has occupied this position since before the Cultural Revolution. Under him are three vice-chairmen, one from the militia and two from the masses. The Communist Party constitutes a separate, and possibly equally important, power infrastructure; of the seven hundred party members in the commune, nineteen serve on the RC; thus a group constituting less than 3 percent of the commune's population holds 76 percent of the seats on the supreme governing body.

Though the organization of the commune, as we observed it that day at Malu, seemed well entrenched and satisfying to the peasants it served, it has but a short history. We were reminded that, like the Revolution itself, life in the countryside is ever changing and growing. Land reform began immediately upon Liberation in 1949, with confiscation of the vast holdings of the landlords. Each peasant was given his own tiny plot—a guarantee that he himself would receive the benefits of his labor and a most telling step forward in a land-based society. Within a few years most peasants were mired down in a hopeless struggle for livelihood, as they were unable to produce efficiently on a base of millions of individual enterprises. They turned to working together, first in mutual-aid teams and then in cooperatives of various structures, pooling their labor in common plots. Major progress eluded them until 1955 when Mao first proposed communal organization, which by 1958 emerged as the economic base of agriculture. Since then their standard of living has moved steadily

[42]

*Peasants' homes at Malu today include two-storied attached houses, a small shed for animals, and a one-*mu *private garden plot.*

upward. The average annual wage has increased from about 300 to about 500 yuan. All our hosts agreed that, while much of this advance resulted from new methods and diversification, the most important gains arose from the new political consciousness inspired by the Cultural Revolution, the most recent step in the socialization process.

Malu families live in newly constructed, two-story concrete structures, which afford comfortable living space. These are located in villagelike clusters, corresponding to production units. We visited one peasant home for a family of four; it is part of an attached block of six houses constructed cooperatively by the production unit whose specific job at the commune is to build such dwellings. Each of the four rooms is about sixteen feet square; the lower level, including the kitchen and living-dining rooms, has

Many peasants take their meals in brigade canteens.

earthen floors, while the two bedrooms on the upper story have cement floors. The land on which they are built belongs to the commune, but the houses are considered private property, unlike city apartments, which are owned by the state and rented to factory workers. These dwellings cost a family about 1,700 yuan for materials and 120 yuan for the labor of the construction team. A family can save this sum in three to seven years, depending on the number of workers it comprises.

All the newer houses at Malu are equipped with kitchens that are certainly adequate for the preparation of family meals. Nonetheless, many of the peasants prefer to eat at the canteens of their production unit or brigade, which we found to be models of cleanliness and efficiency. Trained workers prepare food of all kinds, much of which is grown on the commune. Certainly our own gastronomic experience at Malu, which included fish, soybean curd, pork, broad beans, egg and vegetable soup, and assorted fruits, was completely satisfactory. This wholesome diet is available in great quantity at the canteen for a total of 12 to 15 yuan per month per person, about one-fourth of the average salary, but since housing and other expenses cost so little, it is perfectly feasible for entire families to take all their meals at these canteens.

Typically, homeowners are provided barn space for chickens, ducks, and a pig, and a small private garden nearby for growing their own vegetables. The family we visited had six chickens and two ducks and therefore enjoyed an ample supply of eggs. They were also fattening a pig, which they could either sell or slaughter. Fuel and grain cost about 5 yuan per month; water and electricity are free; and generally no heating is needed in the Shanghai region, although wood and coal stoves are available. In addition, educational and medical services are widely available and virtually free. Given the annual salary of 500 yuan per laboring person, a family with several working people is assured adequate food, clothing, shelter, and security and can save 300 yuan per year as well.

Unlike farm populations of most Western countries, the peasants of a commune appear to have little desire to migrate to other locations or to move to the city. The normal expectation is to grow up, marry and produce families, and continue to live in the same village. In 1970 the birth rate at Malu yielded about a 2.2 percent increase in the population, or about five hundred to six hundred new babies. There is a national birth control movement that aims to stabilize the population ultimately; the target at Malu is 1.5 percent annual increase, and after a recent educational campaign, half of the more than five thousand women of child-bearing age had adopted some form of birth control. About seven hundred men and eight hundred women had undergone voluntary sterilization after producing families of desired size, and two hundred women now use monthly pills or injections to suppress ovulation. The effective materials in such preparations are apparently of the same type as are used in the Western countries. An additional six hundred to seven hundred women use intrauterine devices, mostly rings.

The average age at marriage on this commune is twenty-five for males and twenty-four for females; the average family has two to three children. Divorces are exceedingly rare, and none at all has occurred on this commune in recent years. If a couple decides to divorce, the commune, through the RC, investigates the matter and makes a recommendation. There is great pressure to keep the family intact. A divorce is taken as a sign of failure not only of

[45]

Food is prepared on a large scale in a canteen at Malu. The molded depressions on the stove top (below) trap heat most efficiently for various sized pots. Kitchen attendants often wear masks (right) to prevent the spread of respiratory infections.

the family in question but of the social unit, the production team to which it belongs. In this case, the double incentive works to reinforce the generally puritanical values that permeate all Chinese mores.

Malu's 27,500 people are engaged in many operations other than pure agriculture. For example, there is a tractor maintenance plant that we toured with Lee Chang-shun, chief of the General Office of the Revolutionary Committee. Here preventive maintenance after every two thousand hours of operation is provided for the numerous tractors owned by the commune. Some are 35-horsepower, standard models built in Shanghai. Others, "walking" tractors, are motor driven but guided by a peasant walking behind them. All forty-three mechanics in this shop had been selected for this work after having been drivers, and had become drivers only after three months of training. Subsequent apprenticeships

One production unit (about 120 workers) operates a tractor repair service at Malu.

A carpentry production team makes small light boats for use on the many waterways at Malu.

for both drivers and mechanics vary in length according to individual candidate's aptitude and preparation and include lectures by graduates of technical institutes.

The chief of the service crew works right on the line with his men. He hurriedly cleaned up his greasy hands when he learned of our approach, and greeted us warmly, his eyes glowing with pride in the excellence of his workmen and their shop. He said that the Malu tractor maintenance plant is so competent that it frequently is asked to handle repair and maintenance of machines owned by other communes. This earns extra work points for the Malu commune and of course increases its income.

In an impressive woodworking shop, buckets and small boats were being made by a staff of what appeared to be expert carpenters. Recently they had learned to cast light concrete boats very cheaply; these are useful on the small waterways (tributaries of the Yangtze) that meander throughout the commune. Some seven hundred such wooden or concrete boats were said to be in use at Malu. We also saw shops for small tool making, machinery fabrication and repair, and a large shop operated jointly with several other communes for building equipment to be used in fertilizer production. Each of these activities was the special responsibility of one production team.

The Chinese may well be the world's best recyclers. Evidence abounded of their successful utilization of all agricultural by-products. We observed many instances of this, like the treatment of sweet potatoes, which are processed at Malu for the manufacture of monosodium glutamate, the widely used flavor enhancer in all Chinese cooking. The waste from this process is fed to pigs, and the by-product ammonia is used to fertilize the fields. In addition, a portion of the harvest is reserved for chemical extraction of the nucleic acids of the cells; these acids are then broken down into their component units and the mixture sprayed onto broad beans (similar to our lima beans) and soybeans for growth improvement. This greatly interested me, since the use in the United States of related chemical growth promoters, called cytokinins, exactly parallels this Chinese practice, which seems to have arisen independently on the basis of farmers' lore, rather than from the laboratory.

Another important product of this commune is soy sauce. The harvested soybeans are pulverized, then mixed with wheat, cooked, stored for eighteen hours at a warm, controlled temperature, and finally fermented by yeast and bottled. The quick method, which takes about three days, requires much yeast, results in an inferior product, and is rarely used. The preferred method takes about forty-five days and produces a rich, flavorful sauce. The residual slag is used as cattle and hog feed, and the waste water for fertilization of the rice fields. No exhortation prompts this useful ecological practice—it is merely everyday routine.

Our tour at Malu took us past a large open shed in which peasants were preparing a cabbagelike vegetable called *dza-tsai* for pickling. In a nearby shed, handsome baskets were being woven from homegrown bamboo. Just beyond that, fences enclosed a pasture where we saw a herd of one hundred and twenty-five fine hybrid dairy cows of mixed Dutch and Chinese stock. Consumption of milk and its products, including cheese, is not customary in China, and cows are less abundant than in Western countries. By contrast, hogs are everywhere, raised by individuals for meat for their own tables and as a communal effort for sale in

[49]

*An advantage of communal organization is diversified activity.
Peasants often prepare food for the canteen. Here they are cutting
dza-tsai, a cabbagelike vegetable that will subsequently be pickled.*

the cities. As a by-product, hog manure is considered very valuable.
This pasture at Malu contained two hundred and ninety of the
beautiful Poland-China variety.

Continuing mechanization and increased use of scientific methods, like similar movements all over the country, bring yearly improvement to Malu. We were told that the commune now boasts
twenty-five pumping stations using either 25-, 40-, or 100-horse-
power motors. We visited a station with a 40-horsepower motor
that could irrigate up to two hundred acres—a tremendous gain over
former hand-operated facilities. Most important, the pumps are
manufactured in nearby Shanghai, where production advances will
result in even wider extension of modern irrigation, obviously one
of China's main instruments for food self-sufficiency.

Insecticides are used, especially against aphids in the vegetable
fields; peasants with powered backpack sprayers were making
their way slowly through the fields. Another means of fighting insect
pests depends on the culture of very susceptible plants, like
cotton and spearmint, together with a plant like the onion, which

allegedly repels insects. I saw and heard no scientific basis for this claim, but, as in other parts of the world, it seems to be widely believed.

The favorite cooking oils in China are rapeseed, sesame seed, cottonseed, and, occasionally, soybean. Rape and barley are grown in rotation on this commune, and yields seemed abundant. By-products of the pressing of rapeseed for the removal of the oil are used for alcohol production; the small distillery that we saw served once again to add to communal profit. Adjacent to the distillery, a small chemical-testing laboratory specialized in uniting sodium carbonate and sulphur to make sodium sulphate, used for dyes, antiseptics, and foodstuffs. Necessary raw chemicals for this operation are purchased from a Shanghai chemical works; the product is sold to the government monopoly.

As a plant physiologist, I noticed with special interest a factory producing the plant growth hormone gibberellin. Here a team of scientists and peasants mix equal parts of wheat and rice chaff with some corn flour, then they cover the mixture with spores of the gibberellin-producing fungus. After several weeks of incubation in what appeared to be bakers' ovens, the fungus mass is skimmed off, its mycelium dried in the sun, ground, mixed with water, and filtered through clay. When sprayed on barley and rape, the product increases yields and, used on cotton plants, protects against the shedding of bolls. This finding should interest agriculturists in the West but needs documentation in acceptable published form. The novelties introduced by the Chinese include the use of the crude product, rather than a crystalline material,

These workers at Malu's gibberellin factory are filling bottles with a mash mixture, the starter culture on which the hormone-producing fungus will be grown—the first step in production of a plant growth enhancer.

The soil is ready. The supports are in place. This large field will soon be planted with beans.

and its use at flowering time, rather than at seedling stage, as is done in the West. The scientist-peasant team also cooperated on other experiments, one of which involved specially composted garbage, which they mixed with nitrogen-fixing microorganisms and applied to the soil to increase crop yields.

Rounding out life at Malu are its schools and hospitals, all located within and run by the commune itself. Children thus attend school on the commune until the age of sixteen—through nursery school, kindergarten, primary school, and lower-middle school. A selected number then go on for an additional two years of training in upper-middle school, and a still smaller number, after several years of employment in factory, commune, or army, attend the universities. Most graduates of higher education return to the commune where their new knowledge can be used to "serve the people."

[52]

As for medical facilities, each brigade boasts a well-equipped outpatient clinic, and the commune has a large modern hospital with all the facilities usually found in a provincial center. In addition, each production team has its own health station with "barefoot doctors" and such other paramedical personnel as midwives, herb specialists, and acupuncturists to handle minor problems and preventive medicine.

Recreation and the spiritual life are more difficult for a Westerner to assess, especially without knowledge of the language. We noticed arenas where home talent shows and plays or movies by traveling road troupes were said to take place. Athletics and exercise programs, widely available and popular all over China, provide further diversion. Literature is severely curtailed, and the news and music blaring hourly on loudspeakers yield little knowledge of the outside world. But the Chinese peasant, at least on the Malu commune, doesn't appear to suffer from these deficiencies. He is too busy enjoying his newly gained prosperity.

His well-being stems from organization and diversification that have developed a wonderfully effective life style, in which each peasant can participate: he votes for officials; he assists in work plans; he sees the results in direct returns to himelf and his family. It is easy to understand his enthusiasm for the new regime and the innovations of the Cultural Revolution; the system in Old China, under which all land and produce belonged to the landlords, health care and schools were nonexistent for peasant families, and individual dignity was brutalized, still lives in bitter memories. Peasants today recognize fully the leaps and bounds they have taken; they are justly proud, and they are perfectly reasonable in believing that the quality of their material lives will continue to improve.

What I saw and observed in one day in 1971 at the Malu People's Commune dominated all other impressions in its implications for an understanding of the New China. From that day on, an extended communal experience became the objective of my further travels in China.

Shih Chen-yu, 73, and his wife Sun Shu-zheng, 69, were our hosts during a two week visit at Lugou Ch'iao People's Commune near Peking. They shared with us not only the facilities of their home but the rich and varied daily activity within it as well.

4

From Pedant to Peasant

A T 9 : 0 0 A . M . on Monday, June 19, 1972, Dale, Beth, and I
shouldered small bags containing our essential clothes and toilet
articles and set out for two weeks of life and work on a commune. It was an important step for us, not only because living on
the commune was the focus of our trip to China, but also because
achieving it on our terms represented an extraordinary compromise
for our hosts. Contrary to all their notions of proper hospitality,
they had arranged for us to be accepted as working members of
a production team on the Lugou Ch'iao Jen'min Gungsha, the
Marco Polo Bridge People's Commune. Our sole companion was
our friend and interpreter, Li Ming-teh. And what good fortune
for us, as his warmheartedness and engaging sense of humor made
him very easy to be with, and his common sense continually
expedited our movements without fuss. For his part, he claimed
to be delighted at the opportunity to spend some time in the
country, which he said he much prefers to the city.

After a friendly leavetaking of Mr. Hsu of the arrangements
committee in Peking, we walked about three blocks to a bus stop
and took our places in the waiting line amid the curious stares
of the bustling, early-morning crowd. Beth and Dale were dressed
in the Chinese fashion—shiny new cotton pants, square-cut Mao-
type cotton jackets, and gigantic *tsao mao* (peasant straw hats),

procured the evening before at a Peking department store, in the midst of other shoppers who reacted with gales of laughter to the sight of Westerners in such headgear. I was wearing work pants and a short-sleeved shirt with my *tsao mao* dangling down my back from its string around my neck. Our presence puzzled the Chinese in the line; they are used to seeing foreigners in Peking, but not to seeing them use public transportation.

The electric trolley bus arrived within three minutes, and we piled aboard. It was crowded but, magically, seats became vacant. We arranged our luggage into a small pyramid and grouped ourselves in four seats around it. In the midst of the hubbub and chatter of our fellow passengers, we began to feel closer to the people than we had before. Most of them gazed at us curiously; some stared fixedly with impassive faces; others smiled when we smiled.

We rode on three buses during our trip of about twenty kilometers to the southwest of Peking. At each bus stop, at each boarding, the procedure was the same. We aroused much curiosity, we were greeted by stares, smiles, politeness, and we were offered seats. By the time we had settled into the third bus, Peking had begun to sprawl into the flat countryside, and the crowds had thinned out considerably, making it possible for us to get a better view out of the windows. There streamed the bicyclists, pedaling with great dignity and deliberateness in either direction. A few cars, trucks, and buses punctuated the otherwise silent flow of traffic with their horns and engine noise. Children played on the streets before workers' apartment houses, and in at least two places the game they played looked suspiciously like hopscotch. We passed one building where a long line of people waited to purchase tickets for an athletic event to be held that evening. As we rode farther into the suburbs, we could see the road stretching far ahead of us, edged on both sides with a continuous line of trees. This is typical of Chinese roads, for a massive tree-planting effort has transformed the appearance of rural China. These lines of poplars and camphor trees also serve as windbreaks and welcome shade to temper the hot, midsummer climate.

The final stage of our bus journey, which took almost two hours, with changes and waiting, paralleled the new subway system, recently built and put into service in Peking. According to Li, it is merely an east-west line and so far provides only limited service, but plans have been made for extending its routes and thereby its usefulness.

Quite suddenly, at a bend in the road, the bus stopped, and we were told that this was as close as it could get to Lugou Ch'iao Commune; we would have to walk the last kilometer. It was hot and sticky (Peking gets about 70 percent of its annual precipitation during the summer when the mean temperature is eighty degrees). And burdened as we were, anxious as we were, the distance loomed much farther. We walked slowly, stopping frequently to mop the perspiration and to change hands, as our fingers numbed from carrying even the reasonably light bags we had packed. By now we were walking alongside farm fields planted mainly in vegetable crops—acres of tomatoes, eggplants, cucumbers, and beans. In the distance we could see cornfields, and we learned later that there were extensive rice and wheat plantings as well. The traffic was mainly on foot. Farmers, schoolchildren, and mothers with children by the hand stopped and stared at us curiously as we approached and passed them. The stares seemed more open, frank, and friendly than those in the city. The good broad peasant faces didn't need much encouragement before the mouths turned up into a smile. This tendency must have been compounded by the rather ridiculous appearance we presented. Certainly nothing like us had ever hit their region before.

After about twenty minutes, we were approaching two small villages. Li, who had been brought up in the countryside, paused occasionally to ask directions. The answers at first seemed ambiguous to him, but as we got closer to the village of our destination, the answers became more certain. Yes, we were heading in the right direction. Yes, they had heard about our coming, and we were expected.

Finally, we turned off the paved road onto a dusty, red-soil lane that cut between the rear edge of a row of village houses and a thriving tomato field. We had not proceeded more than a minute or two when we heard a burst of commotion from within one of the compounds, and immediately a short, sturdy, smiling woman in baggy trousers, white blouse, and *tsao mao* hurried out to meet us and introduce herself. Chang Shu-men seemed a dynamo of energy; she chattered exuberantly with Li and pumped our

[57]

*Our life at Lugou Ch'iao was enriched by the guidance and human-
ity of these friends. Here with my daughter Beth at left are Li
Ming-teh, our interpreter, Syao Chang, head of women's work
for our production unit, Lao Chang, head of the production unit,
and Syao Tsui, another interpreter.*

hands vigorously. After her welcome, we again picked up our
bags and followed her on down the lane toward the compound
in which we were to stay. On the way we were joined by another
smiling peasant, Chang Chung, the leader of Mei Shih Kou Production Team, a *syao dwei* (little unit) of the Syao Tuen Brigade,
the *da dwei* (large unit) with whom we would work.

When we entered the compound, we were surrounded by what
seemed a huge crowd, all of them talking constantly and excitedly and gazing at us with undisguised delight and interest. We
were led to the house we were to occupy, where we deposited our
belongings. Cold water was then drawn into enameled pans from a
hand-operated pump in the center of the courtyard, mixed with
some hot water from a teakettle, and brought to us. With this and
the washcloths, soap, and rinse water we were given, we got rid
of most of the grime of the trip and returned to the courtyard
to join our new friends. There, seated on small stools, we were

served the first of many offerings of tea and smokes. Although this was a regular workday, some of the peasants had taken time to come to chat with us and to make us welcome.

Our hosts were Shih Chen-yu and his wife Sun Shu-zheng. Shih is a stately, slender, ascetic-looking patriarch of seventy-three. Sun Shu-zheng, whose stiff gait draws immediate attention to her tiny, once-bound feet, still shows that in her youth she was an extremely beautiful woman. They have five children, three sons and two daughters, all now married, and twenty-two grandchildren. Two sons and a daughter live on the commune, while one son and a daughter live in Peking as factory workers. Each of the sons on the commune is now the head of his own family; the elder has moved into another compound nearby, and the younger, with his wife and four children, occupies one of the three houses in our compound. It was the latter's wife, Chang Shu-mei, who did most of the hustling and serving within our compound. Ordinarily, she would work at least part time in the fields, but during the year of our visit, because her father-in-law was seventy-three, regarded by the Chinese as a crucial year in an old man's life, she remained on the compound to relieve Shih of his cooking duties. Shih himself no longer goes to the fields to work because of his age. By no means inactive, however, he takes general charge of many of the practical activities of the compound, though overall management rests on the shoulders of his wife, whose quiet firmness insures efficiency.

Chang Chung and Chang Shu-men, who are not related, are the leaders of our production unit, Chang Shu-men being number two in authority and director of the women's work. The two of them became our mentors and fast friends at Lugou Ch'iao. To distinguish between the two Changs, the peasants had nicknamed them Lao (old) and Syao (little). Lao Chang's extreme vigor at only forty-four might seem to belie this designation, but it was no misnomer, for, as Li explained, *lao* is generally used as an indication of respect. It was therefore with some pride that we heard later on that I had been dubbed Lao Gao (*gao,* or tall, being the first symbol in our Chinese name), in keeping with which Beth was called Syao Gao (little tall)—our first "in" joke.

From the very start, our acceptance into the commune was heartwarming. We were eager to start working, but our hosts

Family compounds are built in rows along narrow lanes that open onto larger streets. All are flanked by double rows of trees. At the end of this street is a concrete road leading toward Peking on the left and on the right after half a mile to the stores and clinic building of our brigade.

seemed determined to ease us into our duties. How right they were, we discovered later, as we found ourselves unable to keep up the rigorous dawn-to-dusk routine they take as a matter of course. Thus our first day was spent in orientation, walking around the village to get acquainted with people and places.

The homes of the people in our production team are clustered together in the setting of an old village. (In general, production units coincide in both locality and population with established rural communities.) There are about ninety-seven families and four hundred and fifty people, and together they cultivate five hundred *mu* (eighty-three acres), about two-thirds in produce for the Peking market, the other third in grain, chiefly wheat but including a small rice paddy. All the houses stand within walled compounds arranged in even rows along dirt lanes that form small and large streets. A central square contains the public buildings, four small stores, and the grain yard for wheat thrashing and winnowing, a focus of much of the hard work and pride of the little community.

Unlike the residents of Malu, the peasants at Lugou Ch'iao live in separate houses built by themselves and take their meals with their own families rather than in a central canteen. Although most of the houses have been constructed since Liberation in 1949, they are all one-storied and adhere to the low, spacious tradition of Chinese peasant architecture. They are rectangular, about twenty by forty feet, of gray brick or cement blocks with red tile roofs, punctuated here and there by slender chimneys topped with whimsically designed tile covers. Groups of related houses are enclosed by a cement or brick wall, about six feet high, so that each extended family has a sort of compound for its private living quarters. The compound of Shih Chen-yu and his family, which extends about ninety by eighty-four feet, is divided by a similar cement and brick wall into two courtyards. The entrance from the lane goes into the outer courtyard (twenty-eight by ninety feet), through which we had to pass to enter the larger (fifty-six by ninety feet) inner courtyard—a scene of unending activity and the core of our singular experience.

Remembered now, just as upon entering that first day, it is the very strangeness that makes that courtyard scene so vivid. The well is the hub. Someone is always pumping water—into buckets, bowls, or jars—for washing, cooking, or cleaning. And the busy-

The inner courtyard hums with activity. Here Syao Chang pumps water while Chang Shu-mei kneads dough.

ness spreads into every corner. Chang Shu-mei plays the genie who makes things happen. Cheerfully in action from morning till night, she prepares and serves food, washes clothes and dishes, sweeps the courtyard, bathes her toddlers in tubs, and if she has an extra moment, makes clothing for her children on the treadle-operated sewing machine, which she carries from our house out into the courtyard. The grandfather takes great pride in caring for the pig, which requires much gathering, chopping, cooking, pickling, and mixing of the feed materials. He also does countless small repair jobs—on the clothesline, the tool shed, and the wheeled carts. Grandmother, though far less active and often busy at accounts and planning, specializes in a rather sly method of baby chick catching. She sits quietly on the stoop in front of her house, watching the confusion that always attends catching the chicks to put them in large baskets for the night. Quick as a cat, she

Grandmother is the expert at braiding garlic. Her hands fly as she works near the rabbit hutches of our inner courtyard.

swoops them up in one hand as the children chase them by her in their more futile attempts. She is an expert as well at making long braids of garlic that are hung quite decoratively to dry on trees and high walls around the inner court.

As the young children come home from school in the late afternoon, each one goes immediately to his or her task as if it were the natural order of the universe that chores be done. Various children bring in vegetables they have gathered in the family plot. One granddaughter always brings in cabbage leaves from the field; she puts them in a corner of the yard and chops them up for the baby chicks to pick at. When they are well picked over and totally dry, she rakes them into a heap and transfers them to a large metal cauldron, where they are mixed with other waste materials, then cooked and prepared for the pig. Another older grandchild always helps the old man carry the heavy pots of feed to the pigpen in the outer courtyard. A grandson, whose regular job is at one of the six factories on the commune, seems to have the special responsibility of keeping the pump in good working order and twice while we were there gave it a thorough going over. He also is forever busy oiling bicycles, repairing flat tires, and tidying up the storage sheds.

Food preparation for such a large, active family is constant, and everyone helps. Someone is always at work at one of the low tables under a tree in the courtyard—cleaning, chopping, or mixing. No one seems ever to have to tell anyone else what to do in this harmonious world, and it was immediately comfortable and satisfying for us to be a part of it.

The three houses are along the west and north walls of the compound. Two of them, built of brick with tile roofs, are approximately twenty-one feet wide by forty feet long and form an L at the northwest corner of the enclosure. The house on the north wall belongs to the old couple, while the house on the west wall, which we occupied, is the home of the number-two son, Shih Ming, his wife, Chang Shu-mei, and their four children. They had most graciously moved out, cleared it for our use, and were somehow managing doubled up in the grandparents' house. Alongside the grandparents' house is a much smaller, apparently older, and more ramshackle house, which an unrelated tenant family is renting while they await completion of an apartment house closer

Grandfather and granddaughter work together. He is directing where she is to rake the cabbage leaf culls for the baby chicks.

After the cabbage leaves have been picked over by the baby chicks, grandfather brews them into feed for the pig, a prized possession. In the background are the fermentation vats used for this process.

to the steel mill where the husband and wife are workers. They, their four children, and a grandmother live in an area that an American couple would find restrictive.

Although number-one son and his family have built their own compound nearby, they continue to take their meals with the old folks and the extended family. Of the other three children, one daughter, a schoolteacher at Lugou Ch'iao, bicycled over three times during our stay, but the two who are factory workers in Peking apparently visit infrequently.

Each of the larger houses is divided into two rooms by walls at right angles to the length of the house. In our dwelling such a wall makes a large room about twenty-eight feet long and a smaller room about twelve feet long. Each has, at one end, a *k'ang,* on which family members sleep at night, sit during the day, store bedding materials, and keep warm during the winter. The source of all this comfort is a raised earthen platform, supported by a brick or stone wall about thirty inches high. It is placed over a fireplace built into the floor; on top of the fireplace is a flue that can be adjusted so that the heat of the stove can be directed either to a small stove for cooking food or brewing tea or into ducts running under the *k'ang.* During the cold winter a wood or charcoal fire burning all night keeps the users very warm while they sleep. The *k'ang* is covered by tightly woven straw mats and is thus kept neat and clean. In addition, we had padded cotton mats to unfold and use as both mattress and quilt. We do not know whether this was a special luxury for us or a general practice. The pillows stuffed with chaff were quite comfortable. If the night was cool, there was a spare cotton mat. We kept an upper window above our *k'ang* open at night. This caused consternation among our hosts, who felt sure the night air would make us sick.

The *k'ang* in our room measures about six feet wide and eighteen feet long. It could (and probably does) accommodate an entire family. Beth's smaller room contains the same sort of *k'ang* and floor stove, but of much smaller dimensions. A partition fashioned of a brick base, topped by wooden lattice work covered with rice paper separates the rooms. The openings between the rooms and to the outside are covered by flexible, matchstick bamboo screens. In addition, a regular wooden door with glass windows opens onto the courtyard.

The wonderful all-purpose k'ang. *Each room in Lugou Ch'iao houses contains one of these large earthen platforms. Heated by a floor fireplace, the k'ang serves as bed, lounge, and storage shelf.*

Sitting on the steps of her house, grandmother helps daddy with a haircut. Then it's bathtime. After use, the water will be carefully spread over the courtyard to help maintain the firm clay floor.

The cement floor becomes dusty very easily from traffic in and out of the house, and cluttered because no one hesitates to drop cigarette butts on it. It is customary to sprinkle water or old tea on it to settle the dust, which is frequently swept up with the debris and deposited in a refuse pile outside. The extremely simple furniture consists of a large worn table, which served us as a desk, between the *k'ang* and the outer door and, on the opposite wall, a chest of drawers and a sewing machine. The area adjacent to the partition separating the two rooms serves as a wash-up center and can be screened off from the rest of the room by pulling down bamboo hangings or towels suspended from the ceiling by bamboo poles. The windows facing eastward onto the courtyard have blue cotton curtains that can be drawn for privacy; we used them only when we were asleep, resting, or washing our bodies.

Bathing is sponge bathing. We adapted to their system of mixing hot and cold water in an enamel pan, bringing it to the waist-high, tripod-supported wooden stand near the wall between our rooms, and washing, rinsing, drying—staying clean without total immersion. The dirty water is carried back out to the courtyard where it is emptied with a swirling motion so as to spread it over as large a surface as possible. This practice keeps the earthen yard packed and relatively dust free. Sometimes the water is carefully poured into the depressions surrounding the trees in the courtyard or around the bases of the flowers or squash plants that are grown in neat bamboo enclosures. Nothing is ever wasted.

The east wall of the inner courtyard is given over largely to cooking sheds. The renting family uses two stoves, one brick and one cement, protected only by an overhanging roof. Our host family has a more finished cooking shed, approximately ten by twelve feet in size. It is covered with a tile roof and enclosed with concrete walls, four feet high, that are connected to the roof with open brickwork. It was almost unbearably hot in the cooking sheds (100 degrees or more) while we were there, but is said to be very snug in colder weather. The fires are started first thing each morning with a handful of straw from a pile kept in the outer courtyard; kindling sticks, then larger pieces of wood, and finally charcoal are piled on. These fires are kept going all day long and, among other advantages, provide a ready supply of hot

[69]

water through the continual use of big teakettles and thermos-style jugs for storage.

The south wall is lined with rabbit hutches and wigwamlike chicken houses, made of long hollow reeds fastened together at the apex by bindings of leaves and closed at the bottom by a metal grillwork door hinged on a vertical post. The rabbit hutches are more substantial, being made of brick and mortar and closed by perforated metal doors. The rabbits are rarely, if ever, let out of their hutches; their diet of vegetables is carried to them and placed inside the door. The fat hens and the rooster, however, enjoy the freedom of the yard for one or two hours every afternoon, after which the children, amidst much excitement, chase them back into their pens. The two dozen baby chicks that peck around the yard most of the day never fail to cause much scrambling and giggling when the children round them up and place them in woven straw containers for the night.

In spite of all the activity, the courtyard is always neat, and indeed, attractive. Each one tidies up his own mess from any cooking or repairing chore immediately. The small fruit trees provide shade and softening greenery, and hollyhocks, chrysanthemums, and geraniums at doorways and on windowsills, touches of color to the human beehive. How much young and old alike value the quality of their lives shows in their willing attention to the simplest or most tedious chore.

Just south of our house on the west wall of the compound is a tool shed in which are stored bags of grain, work implements, several wheeled carts, and the bicycles belonging to the family. Immediately adjacent to that, in the southwest corner of the inner court, is the family toilet. This deep pit lined with concrete has one large opening covered by a concrete slab. It is open to the sky but protected from surface view by a series of bafflelike walls. There is no seat; to use it, one squats. There is no obvious supply of paper, but forewarned, we had brought several rolls of toilet paper from Peking. The peasants generally manage without toilet paper, using odd scraps of paper available from many sources.

Human waste is used with great profit in China and other Oriental countries. In fact, it is doubtful whether their agriculture could proceed very long without it, in view of the relative shortage of synthetic fertilizers. When the concrete-lined toilet is nearly

Beth and some of the children help to braid garlic. They are seated near the opening to the outer courtyard. The rabbit hutches are in the right background and a corner of the chicken teepee shows in the right foreground.

full, it is emptied, either by long shovels and buckets or by a truck with a suction hose. The manure is then transported to a large concrete storage tank (one of several provided for the brigade) where it is tightly sealed to ferment anaerobically for two to three months. During this time the obnoxious odors disappear, and because of the elevated temperatures produced during fermentation, harmful spores and cysts are killed. When the material is withdrawn, it is diluted with irrigation water and applied directly to the fields. So far as is known, the health hazards associated with the use of human manure have been minimized by the Chinese. Certainly what we learned of the health system, and what we observed of the people, led us to believe that they do not suffer from intestinal parasites, although some organisms might possibly survive the fermentation procedure. Such a technique probably could be adopted profitably in the United States and other countries wishing to put wastes to good use instead of dumping them into the rivers and the sea.

Between the large cooking shed and the rabbit hutches of our courtyard, an opening in the wall leads to the outer courtyard. Here, in a splendid concrete enclosure, lives the family pig, an efficient converter of waste material into useful and edible products. Each family in the village always has at least one pig. Procured as piglets and fattened over several months, they are then either slaughtered for consumption by the family or sold and the profit used for purchasing other food. Pig manure serves as a highly valued fertilizer in the vegetable fields. Thus, recycling of waste from our courtyard is, quite literally, complete.

Near the pigpen is a small shed for a ewe and her lamb. The ewe is tethered and the lamb, which is still suckling, is permitted to ramble. It frequently invades the inner courtyard, where it delights in pursuing the chickens. This always produces a great flurry, a good bit of dust raising, and frantic cackling. Finally one of the children simply brandishes a stick and frightens the lamb back into the outer courtyard.

The remainder of the outer courtyard is occupied by storage piles of straw, coal, charcoal, and wood. Here the father of the renter family fabricates the coal balls that are used in the stoves. Finely pulverized coal and mud are mixed with water to form a slurry, which is molded into rectangular boxes about two inches

Shih Chen-yu pours food for the pig in his magnificent concrete-lined stall in the outer courtyard.

The ewe and her lamb (below) occupy a simpler shed in the outer courtyard.

high. These are then sliced into small cubes and permitted to dry in the sun. Care in measuring the correct proportions of coal and mud for these briquettes insures the hot, yet slow-burning flame necessary for cooking.

A variety of materials compose the wall surrounding our compound. Smooth, weathered cement, like most other commune walls, dominates, but red brick lengths reinforce certain areas, and behind the pigpen, a stretch of the original earthen wall still stands. Historically, all the houses in the village had been built with such mud walls, which served well until a deluge of rain occurred. At such times, paradoxically, the peasants would have to leave the shelter of their homes for fear that the mud walls might collapse on them. While walking in the village our first day, we saw such a mud house surrounded by a mud wall. It used to be the most luxurious house in the village, but now it is maintained as a historical curiosity.

Our family had been able to save enough to build all three of their houses in the ten years between 1954 and 1964 (and since then had saved another 1,000 yuan). Our house, built in 1954, shows no major signs of deterioration. Certainly the plaster walls inside need painting, and the cement floor has cracks here and there, but the architecture is so simple and the supporting beams,

Almost all homes at Lugou Ch'iao now have brick walls. Formerly, all walls were mud, like this one behind the pigpen at the home of our host family.

wall structure, and roof tiles so sturdy and well maintained that it is expected to last a hundred years or more. Welcomed into that home and its many strengths, we no longer felt like outsiders in China.

Even then, when life for Shih and his family was so shaken up by our arrival, we were aware of the rigidity of their daily routine. Just before 5:00 A.M., everyone gets up to the sounds of "The East Is Red" broadcast by loudspeakers over the whole commune and followed by the official morning news. After a quick wash-up and a cup of tea, everyone goes to the fields and works from about 5:30 until 7:00. Then it is time for a real breakfast back in the courtyard, followed by a brief rest. Work takes up again at about 8:00 or 8:30 and continues until noon with only a twenty- or thirty-minute break at about 10:00. Lunch, the big meal of the day, at 12:00, is followed by a longer rest period during the hot hours of the day until 2:00 or 2:30. Work continues until about 7:00 P.M. with one or two short rest periods. Some of the peasants, especially during the busy season, return to the fields in the evening for extra labor. This is considered volunteer labor, though there are strong social pressures for each person to take his turn. And in time of such emergencies as the need for daily irrigation during a drought, one-third of the work force would be on duty each night as well. It is difficult to see how these people retain their strength and cheerfulness during these long working days and not too restful nights, but they seem to do so.

During the winter the workday is reduced to about four hours, releasing time for a little leisure, some adult education, and maintenance of equipment, but for the eight months of the growing season this demanding, grueling schedule is observed without a day of rest. Sundays merge into the rest of the week, and the rhythm of their work carries the peasants along like a great stream. Even our visit, clearly as extraordinary an event in their lives as in ours, occasioned few interruptions in commune routine.

This, then, became the way we too spent our days at Lugou Ch'iao. I usually awoke easily and went immediately to the well in the courtyard for wash water. Inevitably I was met by Shih, who had been up for some time. He would offer me a teakettle of hot water, and together we would greet another new day. After wash-up he would sit with us on tiny six-inch-high stools at a low round table in the courtyard for tea and a smoke. Li, who slept in another compound, would not have joined us yet, but it did not matter that we had no interpreter to define our remarks; Shih sensed our goodwill and was pleased to share his with us; our feeling of belonging was thereby steadily enhanced. Like many Chinese, he was a fanatic smoker. In fact, a good part of the family's private garden (1 *mu,* or ⅙ acre) was given over to growing tobacco. He was very proud of the beautiful 100-year-old pipe that he had inherited from his grandfather—"so much finer than pipes made today"—which had a jade mouthpiece, a long, slender, cherry wood stem, and a bronze bowl.

We took our meals with the family, rather than in a communal dining room as we had anticipated, and this pleased us, for we valued most the experiences we shared with them. Their simple, daily fare consisted mainly of what was grown on the commune. It was therefore considerably less varied and more monotonous than we were used to eating in city hotels, but nonetheless nutritious and appetizing, good wholesome food to grow healthy bodies.

Central to every meal is an abundance of some starchy food, usually rice or noodles made from wheat flour. In the wheat culture region of northern China, which includes Lugou Ch'iao, noodles take precedence over rice, but both are used. Each person has a deep porcelain bowl into which a layer of rice or noodles is placed. Then, dipping *kwai-tse* (chopsticks) into larger bowls placed in the center of the table, each serves himself portions of a variety of other foods. These included string beans always, since our visit coincided with the peak of their harvest, simply boiled or perhaps pickled or marinated in soy sauce; cauliflower, cabbage, peppers, and cucumbers, usually chopped and eaten raw; squash, also in abundance, and tomatoes. The latter are eaten raw, sprinkled with sugar. The squash is boiled and usually tossed with soy sauce and pork fat. Little bits of meat, often pork, sometimes lamb, rarely beef, are added to some of the vegetable dishes to reinforce the flavor and the protein intake. Vinegar is always served, and whole garlic cloves provided as a side dish "to keep us healthy." Seeing the number-one and number-two sons wolf down two or three great bowls of this mixture was a continual astonishment. Only knowledge of the physical demands of their work made it seem at all possible.

At our main meal, lunch, we were usually served, in addition, a delicious chicken noodle soup, and sometimes, steamed bread. *Woutou* are steamed, partly hollow cornmeal cones that look like little straw hats, a breakfast treat; *laobing* is a large flat wheat loaf; and *mantou* is a rounded, doughy-seeming wheat loaf that looks raw but turned out to be soft, yielding, and moist when bitten into. There is no dessert, though we once had some little sweetened cakes at breakfast. Meals always end with tea and cigarettes. Since everyone smokes, I did too. I tasted five brands with and without filters, of light and dark tobaccos. All resembled similar brands available in the U.S., though slightly more astringent. The dark, moderately strong tea surprised us, since tea we had tasted in the cities tended to be green and weak. We learned later that green tea is more expensive.

We ate leisurely at a table in the main room of the old folks' house, sitting in what were surely the old couple's own highly prized chairs of carved wood with high backs and arms. They were usually placed so that we were seated sidewise to the table. At first we leaned over to one side in order to reach the food, but after a while, since this was really too awkward, we were emboldened to turn our chairs so that we could face the table. Our hosts quickly caught on to our custom, and from then on placed the chairs accordingly. We were almost always joined at the table by Shih or his wife and one or both sons. The rest of the family would sit on the *k'ang,* smoking or drinking tea, waiting until we had finished, at which time they would come to the table and eat some of our leftovers, together with fresh supplies of food brought hot from the cook shed. Sometimes the leftovers were taken outside to the children or other members of the family, who were eating in the courtyard at the little tables we used for morning tea.

We discovered that the Chinese like to see their guests eat quantities of food, and they were always disappointed that we could not consume as much as they did. We would struggle manfully through our bowls of noodles and vegetables only to find that mysteriously they were full again. The old lady was a veritable

Some of the children wait to be served their dinner at the small tables in the inner courtyard. In the right background are recently allotted bags of wheat and at center back the entrance to the family toilet.

"Jewish mother" and reached over with her chopsticks to refill my bowl at the slightest opportunity.

We felt somewhat guilty at this special treatment and, with Li's help, tried to communicate this feeling to our hosts. Why couldn't all of us eat together? Well, it just was not done that way. Why couldn't the others eat first and let us wait once in a while? We were guests and had to be served first. There seemed to be no graceful way out of the situation, and so we accommodated to our hosts' desires. At the cry of *chrfan* (food), we would proceed to our table, and as we departed we would say *chrlebau* ("I have eaten till I am satisfied"). Then we were told to *sushiba* ("take a little rest") on our *k'ang,* although everyone else was washing pans, tending the chickens, chopping up cabbage, tending the sheep, or hauling water.

Frequently, during our rest period, the old lady or old man would arrive, uninvited, in our room with a teapot. After making the tea with the hot water from our stove, they would scald all the cups with the hot tea, throw the residue onto the floor, then pour us a cup, and sit down to join us. This act, typical of life on the commune, afforded much less privacy than we were used to. Generally, when we pulled the curtains for a rest, it was accepted as a signal that we wanted to be alone.

The delivery of tea seemed to be an exception. At such a moment, Shih never introduced a subject for discussion, but in answer to our queries, he told us much of interest about himself and his village. It was founded about two hundred years ago during the Ch'ing (Manchu) dynasty by settlers from the Shantung Province. It became a commune on August 29, 1958, when it was named Lugou Ch'iao Jen'min Gungsha (Marco Polo Bridge People's Commune) after the nearby historic bridge where the Japanese launched their attack on China in 1937. Shih could not say for sure how long his own family has lived here. His great-grandfather was here—perhaps *his* father came from the city. When Shih was a boy, there were twenty families in the village, all descendants of the three original settlers, Chang, Cheng, and Shih. It was called "the confused village" because it was a wilderness of dust, wind, and poor land. There were only three public wells, and all the houses were mud.

He, his two brothers, and sister had formerly lived in the east-

As soon as they come home from school the older children care for the younger ones.

ern part of the village near his parents' compound. After Liberation, he brought his family to their present courtyard, where they built the village's first brick house in 1954. His second son's family built its house in the same courtyard in 1957, and in 1964 the first son's family moved to its house in an adjoining courtyard. The grandfather's older brother and sister are dead; his younger brother, seventy years old, lives in the village with his thirty children and grandchildren.

Life before Liberation was very hard, although less hard for the grandfather's family than for others. His father had owned three *mu* of land, on which they were able to raise enough food to survive through the autumn, but in winter life became almost unendurable. Villagers could find only three kinds of work: peddling, mule renting, and service to the landlord. During the warm months the grandfather worked independently as a tea peddler and a mule renter, but during the winter he was forced to work for a landlord. He bitterly recalled carrying two fifty-kilogram kegs of wine on his shoulders from the landlord's house twenty kilometers into the city in the icy cold over slippery roads and a wooden bridge. For this he was paid 20 fen (less than 10 cents) and served a bowl of millet adulterated with pebbles at the bottom. They had *k'angs* in their house, but often had no money to buy coal, so they burned straw and wild herbs. They ate coarse corn flour mixed with herbs. Only on New Year's Day did they have white flour.

The grandfather was twenty-one and the grandmother seventeen when they married. Their marriage, the old woman recounted, was arranged by a professional matchmaker. She did not see her husband until after the wedding celebration, when she was carried secretly at night, in veils, from her own village to her husband's house. The tradition of arranged marriages persisted until Liberation. Even now parental authority is very powerful in their village, as is traditional behavior between the sexes. Outward displays of affection are frowned upon. Married couples rarely call their spouses *aijen* (beloved or dear), referring to them instead as "father" or "mother" of my child. Changes are slow but evident. The first two sons of our hosts never saw their wives until the wedding night. The third son and older daughter were introduced by their parents; they had known their mates for several years before marriage. The younger daughter, who was married last May, is of the modern generation; she met her husband-to-be through friends and after several months decided to marry; only then did she ask for her parents' consent. Having heeded Chairman Mao's exhortation to marry late, she is twenty-nine, and her husband, thirty. She now teaches primary school in an adjoining brigade but still retains strong ties with her family and always visits on Sundays and days off.

Thus the Shihs revealed themselves as a family strongly unified by purpose as well as bonds of affection. Though they themselves might give all the credit to the leadership of Chairman Mao, to us it seemed that their nation's rebirth depended largely on the spirit and fortitude of families like theirs.

Haystacks symbolize plenty the world over.

5

Working in the Fields

ON OUR SECOND DAY at Lugou Ch'iao we were introduced to *laodung*, or manual labor. Beth and I were assigned first to the grain yard to help in the threshing and winnowing of the wheat. Shrewdly the peasants judged that Dale, somewhat less capable of hard physical labor, would prefer a quieter activity. As she wanted to observe child care facilities because of her professional interests, they assigned her to the seed-sorting shed adjacent to the nursery school compound. Her working companions were other older women and, from time to time, village children. Her work was to separate healthy-looking seeds from wrinkled ones, the vigorous from the aborted.

The grain yard is at once excessively active and incredibly beautiful. Mule-drawn wagons rumble in from the fields laden with golden sheaves that have been cut by scythe or sickle. The loads are dumped into huge piles near the electrically operated threshing machines. These primitive devices, connected to central power hookups, consist of nothing more than open hoppers into which the grain-heavy ends of the stalks are inserted to be chopped up coarsely and thrown onto a belt circling two rollers at high speed. The resulting grain and chaff mixture sprays into the air, and as the machine has been set athwart the wind, the heavier kernels go straight ahead while the lighter chaff is blown cloud-

Helping in the wheat yard proved highly satisfying work. The hopper (right center) has been set across the wind, so that when the grain and chaff are spewed forth the heavier grain tends to go forward and the lighter chaff, to be blown aside.

Many passes through the hopper are required to separate the grain from the chaff. Men and women stand ready to further the process by raking the chaff into one pile, the grain into another. In the picture below a peasant is flicking chaff off the grain pile with a broom made of twigs.

The grain is going through the hopper for the last time leaving a pile of pure wheat. The rolled-up mats in the background are kept handy to cover the grain in case of a sudden rain.

like off to one side. Thus a production line of continual activity is formed in this sea of gold: some peasants stuff the sheaves into the machine, others rake partly separated grain and chaff into piles, while still others gather loads of partly separated grain to be put through another threshing or winnowing process. Because of the relative inefficiency of this operation, it takes seven or eight winnowings before the grain is declared reasonably clean. Between each winnowing, peasants sweep with long brooms fashioned of twigs; a light graceful motion sends the chaff in one direction, and a heavier swipe in the opposite direction adds to the ever-growing, ever-cleaner pile of useable grain.

When the chaff has been worked over several times and is free of grain, it is loaded by means of long pitchforks onto a horse-drawn wagon to be transported to a straw-storage pile. The pitchforks are tools of great elegance. They are not manufactured but rather cut from specially grown trees that are trained to develop three branches at one node. One branch is allowed to grow straight, and the other two are bent out to form right angles, which are later angled again to parallel the central prong. When six-foot-long sections are cut from the trees and the bark removed, they become wonderfully light, supple pitchforks of high tensile strength. With them one can dig into a pile of hay and with one easy graceful motion deposit it on top of a wagon—they help make the work a positive pleasure.

Moving the heavy piles of grain from one threshing machine to another or from the piles into the machines is much harder work. Such loading is accomplished either with wooden shovels, which is not too difficult, or, more frequently, with woven, handle-less trays that resemble large dustpans. Many pounds of grain can be carried in such a tray, and after several hundred rounds of stooping, thrusting the tray into the pile, rising as from a deep knee bend, walking to the machine, dumping the grain, and returning for another load, Beth and I were very tired indeed. We had to pause frequently for breath, while the peasants, in spite of their slight stature and seemingly light musculature, simply continued until the official rest period.

Only once was work in the grain yard interrupted—and then by a flight of jets. The peasants dropped everything, watched intently until the last roar trailed away and, visibly impressed, stopped work to talk it all over. Though we knew jets are uncommon, we did feel this was an overreaction. Li smiled at our puzzled faces and enlightened us. "It's Mr. Henry Kissinger." He then went on to explain that news of Kissinger's expected arrival in Peking had been broadcast all morning on the commune loudspeakers. The peasants had been looking forward to a glimpse of the planes and were not disappointed.

Work in the grain yard was our most regular and most satisfying activity. We took joy in working with the peasants, singing, bantering, jostling, and sharing their pride in the good harvest. Despite a rather dry year, the harvest was considerably better than usual, apparently because of the commune's improved irrigation pumps drawing from subterranean water sources.

Finally the clean golden grain stood piled in the center of the immaculate yard the size of a football field, with the chaff neatly stacked around the periphery. The tools had been cleaned and assembled in sheds around the field, and preparations were made for division of the harvest. The day before that operation, however, a rainstorm threatened. The peasants wasted no time speculating about such an eventuality. They immediately gathered up the tightly woven straw mats that had been piled in a corner of the field. Unfurled, each was about six by ten feet. They laid the mats over the wheat pile in overlapping shingles, building up from bottom to top. In any storm but the most torrential, the water would run off this tightly woven straw covering onto the ground, thus keeping the grain dry.

They employed a similar trick for the straw, which was destined for the piggeries and for the paper and cardboard industries. After the coarse chaff had been piled into a mound about one hundred feet long, six feet wide, and eight feet high, workers gathered the finer pieces into burlap bags, threw them to the top of the pile, where others emptied them so as to fill tightly most of the large holes. This was designed to facilitate water run-off and minimize damage from soaking rains. Sometimes a final step is necessary that involves covering the entire chaff pile with fine clay soil to form an even more protective, water-impervious cover during the rain.

On the day of the division of the production team's own

With handsome pitchforks made from specially grown trees, these women are pitching the chaff into long stacks at the periphery of the grainyard. They manage it with one graceful swoop, though both are small, almost frail-seeming, and have recently given birth.

The peasants bag the grain by filling small, handwoven trays and emptying their contents time after time—a long, backbreaking job.

Each bag is weighed, then closed. An accounting secretary keeps a running total with the aid of an abacus.

portion of the wheat, the yard buzzed with a special excitement. All the family heads were there. The clean wheat was shoveled into heavy burlap bags, which were then closed tightly with binding twine. Each bag was weighed on a balance suspended between two peasants' shoulders and its weight noted in an account book by a recording secretary, who also carried an abacus for keeping a running total. When the entire harvest had been bagged in this way, it was divided—part of it intended for the annual provision for each family and part of it bound for a central grain warehouse and subsequent sale to the Peking market through a government monopoly.

Profit from that sale would ultimately provide part of our peasant friends' yearly income. They had toiled many months, the culmination was a success, and they looked forward to a corresponding profit increase. As at Malu, each individual's share would be determined according to the formula worked out by the production team itself. There would of course be bonuses for superior workers and decreased shares for those adjudged to have contributed less than the average worker, surely resulting in disappointment for some peasants. Having observed the effects of the combined group and individual incentives in the high performance standards of our fellow workers, we found it difficult to imagine much discrepancy in their rates of pay. And that any individual would raise an objection to his allotment in the face of those with whom he lived and worked so closely, who held a common opinion of the value of his labor, seemed practically impossible.

On this day, though, such matters were still in the future. The individual householders swung their family's allotment of two big bags of wheat onto small handcarts and trundled them off to the storage sheds in their own compounds. The bags of grain destined for the community granary were hoisted by two men up on top of horse-drawn wagons. I helped with this lifting job, and for my labors received the most welcome reward of a thumbs-up sign from my fellow workers.

Meanwhile the harvested grain fields were not neglected. Each family was permitted to glean the fields and to process the grain thus acquired for a supplemental supply of wheat. In our compound the children did the gleaning, and the grandmother of the renter family performed the laborious hand threshing and win-

[93]

Finally, each head of family receives his allotted bags of the treasured wheat. Lao Chang triumphantly wheels his home with the help of his small son.

nowing. She emerged triumphantly after several days' work with almost half a bag of extra grain. The peasants call the wheat their "treasure"—and we know it to be so.

Beth and I also worked several days at transplantation of rice seedlings. Since the rice paddies were about a kilometer from our compound near the steel factory at the edge of the commune, we borrowed bicycles and pedaled over the bumpy lanes with Lao Chang as our guide.

Again in the rice fields, the care expended to keep them not only productive but beautiful to behold created an unforgettable scene. Each paddy field had been carefully confined by leveed walls, molded by hand and by shovel into a watertight enclosure. Then, after being flooded, the fields were worked over thoroughly by ox-drawn plows and harrows until the bottom was a uniformly soft, spongy mud, suitable for the nurturing of the tiny seedlings to be planted. These were now about six inches high and a rich green color. Our job was to walk onto the small paths surrounding each seed bed and, squatting on our heels, to remove bundles for transplantation to the paddies. This was done by grasping the base of a group of seedlings and, taking care not to damage the roots, gently pulling and loosening them from the earth. Any soil clinging to the roots was rinsed off, and convenient-sized bunches of the seedlings were tied together with pieces of grass leaf. Peasant girls then transported the bunches in wicker baskets, slung

A picture from the Ming Tombs Museum contrasts sharply with today's practice. The scene shows the peasants in the old days rising up against the landlords who seized so much of the grain for themselves that the peasants had not enough to feed their children.

[95]

Even school children help when it's time to remove rice seedlings for transplantation (above).

The bunches of rice seedlings are carefully separated (below) and thrust down into the mud of the newly flooded paddy.

over bamboo poles on their shoulders, to the nearby fields that were ready for the transplanting. There, women in broad straw hats, standing almost knee-deep in chilly, murky water, deftly separated each seedling and thrust its roots into the mud. The day's work produced a whole new field of evenly spaced seedlings protruding above the water, ready for renewed growth. It was rewarding, joyful work, but for me, painful as well, for my American muscles were not adapted to prolonged heel-squatting. Early on, however, Lao Chang produced a low stool that he had brought along in anticipation of my difficulty. I worked on in relieved comfort, much to the amusement of the peasants.

Several groups of schoolchildren from one of the commune's middle schools helped with the transplantation. These students came to the fields for half a day's labor per week. They were a jolly lot, seemingly much more interested in us than were the older workers. One day, when we were resting in the shade of some poplars between the rice paddies and a cornfield, they broke into song and after several renditions challenged us to respond with some American songs. So Beth and I sang some old-time favorites: "The Blue-Tailed Fly," "Clementine," "My Bonny Lies over the Ocean," and "Old MacDonald Had a Farm." The latter was clearly a favorite; they loved the nonsense of the animal imitations, especially the pig, which made them crack up with laughter. In fact, after several days, "E, I, E, I, O" became the signal for another round of songs.

And in the compound, too, music strengthened our growing friendships. I had brought along my flute and occasionally before dinner played for a while. At the first note, the children gathered around, watching every movement of my hands and lips. They insisted that Beth and Dale sing along, and after a while joined in on the repetitive choruses as the songs became familiar. Beth's harmonica, as well, was a signal for the children to gather. Dale sometimes sang softly to the little ones in the courtyard. She interspersed her music with impromptu English lessons, whereby young and old alike soon learned the English words for nose, eyes, ears, chin, mouth, hair. We, in turn, learned some useful everyday Chinese words, a great addition to the meager vocabularies gained during our four months' "instant Mandarin" crash course.

The rhythm of communal life engulfed us, and we felt in-

During a rest break in the rice fields, the workers seek out some dry ground and sing together.

creasingly a part of it—as though we could continue for a very long time. We were introduced to other types of *laodung:* staking up tomato and cucumber plants; weeding tomato patches; harvesting string beans. The latter operation was carried out in a most lighthearted atmosphere, since it involved so many awkward postures. First, we had to crawl in between the rows of bean vines, supported by bamboo poles, joined at the top and spread apart at the bottom. There we squatted, cramped and perspiring, to pick the beans, which grew thickly in such enclosures. Our baskets were soon full, and we struggled out, dumped the beans into bags at the end of the field, and then had to wriggle back into the teepee-like tunnels for another load. The air rang with the songs and stories and giggles of the young women working there. They teased their production team leader, Syao Chang, for her impetuousness, and she complained about her husband's laziness. She told us that she was married at twenty-four because of parental pressure and now regretted it. Her husband now sits around and plays chess after his factory work, leaving her to do all the housework. Also he wants her to move to the factory in the city, but she likes life and work in the country and feels strongly and enthusiastically that she can best serve the people by remaining there as a "responsible person." And after sharing the company of this attractively cheerful and hardworking young woman for several weeks, we too were confident of her outstanding contribution to her production team.

A special camaraderie pervaded the tomato patch, because only girls who belong to the Communist Youth League work there. Chairman Mao had visited this very patch in 1958 during a tour of China's cooperatives. A month later he issued the directive that transformed all cooperatives into communes. In honor of that memorable event, the field is always planted in tomatoes and always cared for by Communist youths.

During these long, hard days of *laodung*, our willingness to carry a fair share of the load earned us considerable acceptance into the community. Naturally it pleased us to see the early reserve of many of the peasants begin to disappear, and we felt especially rewarded when invited to attend a meeting for political education and criticism.

At Lugou Ch'iao, as in every commune and factory throughout

Tomatoes must be carefully staked up to increase yield, as produce for Peking dinner tables accounts for about two-thirds of the output of our production team.

China, workers must attend political meetings regularly. Our production team held such meetings twice weekly, generally immediately after lunch, before beginning the afternoon's work. Sessions were scheduled for about an hour and a half but sometimes lasted longer. A commonplace event for our peasant friends but certainly not for us! As we anticipated it, the companionship of Li Ming-teh and his sensitive interpretation never seemed more comforting.

The meeting convened around an open shed in the shadow of a building near the grain yard. People sat, reclined, or squatted on their heels. It appeared as though all two hundred workers in our production unit were there; in addition to the adults, many babies were in evidence, some being suckled by their worker mothers. The meeting came to order when one of the peasants stepped out from the crowd and, with the help of printed notes, read a hortatory message about fulfilling the tasks of the harvest and doing the job well. "The chain is only as strong as its weakest link," he said. People listened, but some looked rather glassy-eyed, others had their eyes closed, and a few were even chatting about other matters. At one point, to highlight the necessity for personal sacrifice, the speaker cited the heroism of Norman Bethune, the noted Canadian surgeon and physician, who died while helping the Eighth Route Army after the Long March. As he continued, emphasizing the necessity to coordinate different aspects of the work, some people sipped tea; others just listened, reactionless. They seemed to have heard it all before.

Immediately after he sat down, a political cadre came vigorously forward and, without any notes, harangued lengthily about the almost completed wheat harvest and the barley harvest yet to come. Although he paid tribute to the excellence of the work and the expected abundance, he deplored the commune's lack of total self-sufficiency and annual need to buy additional wheat. He mentioned ways to increase productivity. He went on to the necessity of paying adequate attention to the vegetables, to land management, and to "keeping up the spirit." He extolled some women who "work better than men" as well as those who work extra hours at night. We looked around; the lethargy continued, even in the face of such a spirited speaker; perhaps it was because of the extreme heat.

Old Chang, the production team leader, then rose to talk mainly about the 20 *mu* of sorghum and spring onions. He commended the unselfishness of comrades who worked until 4:00 A.M., then returned to the fields at 5:00. Because of their heroic efforts, he said, 470 *catties* (1 catty = ½ kilogram or about 1.1 pounds) per *mu* will be harvested, an increase of about 15 percent over last year despite the dry year. "All this," he stressed, "is possible with the application of Chairman Mao's teachings." Then, turning to us, "Even American friends have come from afar to help this production team and to make contributions to the work of the commune." He used our presence to entreat the workers to intensify their efforts. "Try to finish the harvest by the end of the month," he said. He closed by asking everyone to emulate our hard work. He asked us, as foreign visitors, for criticism. We declined and he then asked others for their opinions.

In response, a young Communist League woman rose to give what can only be described as a pep talk. She pledged her own high performance, despite the hot and dry weather. Because the coming months of August and September would be even more difficult, she exhorted all to follow the lead of her group. Another woman, caught up in this spirit, rose to add her support. She vowed to overfulfill her task, even though she was still a young girl. "The Communist Party and the Young Communist League members have been in the fore, and we should learn from them."

At this juncture, a husky, bearded worker introduced a new tone into the discussion. "This is fine as far as we have gone but what are the weak points in our performance? Yes, I will criticize the leaders. Grain is the treasure of the peasant, but much is left in the field. We have not been sufficiently careful in bringing out every possible grain. Also not enough attention has been paid to vegetables. Let us pick the fresh tomatoes and cucumbers and other vegetables at their peak for the citizens of Peking."

The criticism implicit in these remarks brought Old Chang to his feet. He admitted certain faults in his own management of the harvest, and he regretted his neglect of the cauliflower, among other things. He observed that some wheat harvesters were careful, while others were not; each man should be master of his own production and try to improve his own performance.

The political cadre rose again to repeat and extend his tirade even more forcibly. He praised the youth leaders for their good work and called on everyone to emulate "the foolish old man," in Mao's famous parable "who managed to move the mountain." Another speaker responded to this new exhortation by pointing out that, despite the dry year, much good work had been performed because of the drainage and irrigation. When I looked around at this point, nothing had changed. Many eyes were glassy, and children were skittering around. I could not tell whether people were bored or impassively thoughtful.

Syao Chang then changed the subject with a complaint about the team's lack of attention to environmental sanitation. She announced that she had some insecticide to fight flies and mosquitoes that was available for use by all. She called it *didiwei,* which we translated as DDV, said to be stronger than DDT. After Syao Chang's words, the meeting drew to a close with the welcome news that, because of the extreme heat, work would not be continued until 5:00 P.M.

We walked back to the courtyard with Old Chang, where we sat in the shade and sipped some tea. He seemed a bit chastened by the criticism of his leadership. "For a man who can't read or write, it is difficult to manage 500 *mu* and 500 people," he said. He thus excused what he called his own poor management of the production team. We reminded him that he was elected as leader and had held his post for nearly fifteen years—ever since the commune was formed. If his performance were poor, wouldn't he be replaced? He smiled and made some comment about all his friends' sensitivity to his feelings. We learned later from others that he is very highly regarded as one of the commune's ablest production-team leaders. His wife complains that he sacrifices so much of his own time and effort for the good of the production team that his own compound is neglected and in considerably worse condition than those of his neighbors. He is also, because of some family reverses, in debt to the production team and, even though the leader, he is paid no more than the average good worker. We tried to press this matter to find out the nature of his troubles, but we had reached a dead end.

We had gone to this meeting with the sure knowledge that such continuing political education is a fact of life in socialist countries, and that was borne out. But we came away with new insights. "Putting politics in command" is indeed a fact of life that has effectively united China in its vast common effort. The peasants know it well, and respect it, but do not feel the necessity to rally constantly around the rhetoric. On the other hand, these meetings afford them a much more precious right—the opportunity to voice their ideas on the issues that affect their lives most directly. The open give and take about the amounts of land to be farmed for each crop, the responsibility for irrigation or field preparation, or the criticism of effort is a model of democratic action—no matter how dictatorial the edicts from Peking on overall production goals. And, given the differences between private and public ownership, the genuine satisfaction potential does not seem too divergent from that of farmers in a capitalistic system. Working together toward such satisfactions—seeing clearly and directly the results of their endeavors—is surely a more potent, if less obvious, unifier than political education.

Three members of the Revolutionary Committee of the duck farm at Lugou Ch'iao stand in front of a poster urging "In agriculture, learn from Tachai." The ubiquitous slogan refers to an especially heroic commune's efforts to form fields out of rocky hillsides.

6

The New Security

OUR REJECTION of the ordinary lines of protocol at the beginning of our stay at Lugou Ch'iao had denied the leaders of the commune the opportunity of proffering what they considered an appropriate greeting. They had conceded, but enough was enough. After a few days a delegation, including Liang Shu-huen, vice-chairman of the Revolutionary Committee of the commune, Juo Jen-yuan, chairman of the Revolutionary Committee of our brigade, and several others paid an official call. In the ensuing discussion, they presented us with additional information about our commune, in particular some figures from which the life-giving effect of nationwide communal organization in 1958 emerged dramatically.

	Summer 1958	*Summer 1972*
Number of people	37,000	46,000, an effect chiefly of the growth within resident families
Land area	42,000 *mu*	37,000 *mu* decreased in area under cultivation caused by increase in area given over to factories, highways, roads, and houses; higher output despite this change.

[105]

	Summer 1958	Summer 1972
Vegetables	1,000,000 *catties*	2,400,000
Grain	700,000,000 *catties*	850,000,000
Pigs	9,000	48,000
Average salary	300 yuan per year	400–600 yuan, depending on productivity of particular enterprise
Medical facilities	None organized; 30 doctors in entire commune area	1 hospital, 21 clinics, and over 450 medical and paramedical personnel
Schools	10 primary; 0 secondary	19 primary; 5 secondary
Housing	Mainly mud, poor	Brick, much improved
Factories	0	6
Seed stations	0	1
Fruit	0	480,000 *catties,* mainly peach, pear, grape, and apple produced by 1 orchard brigade
Irrigation	2–3 *mu* per day, primitive	50 *mu* per pumping station, each with several pumps
Tractors	0	30 riding- and 68 walking-style
Trucks	0	68

After this first visit, Liang and the other officials came frequently to see us—in the fields during rest breaks or back at our compound after the day's *laodung*. On one such visit, Liang described in detail the commune's complex organization. The Revolutionary Committee at Lugou Ch'iao is elected by the masses. This involves, first of all, the selection of three to five members from each production unit for a representative assembly that nominates the candidates every two years. Thirty-three members are then elected.

Currently membership consists of eight women and twenty-five men (nineteen from the masses of workers, eight cadres, and six from the People's Liberation Army). Included in this breakdown are twenty-three Communist Party members, six youths, and several brigade leaders.

Thirteen are considered full-time RC members: eight cadres, five PLA people, no peasants. Even the full-time members are required to work in field or factory at least one day per week—more in the harvest season. The chairman is a woman; she and two other women are among the full-time members. She has been continuously elected to office since 1958. Liang has been vice-chairman just one year; he was formerly a "responsible person" in the commune office.

The Revolutionary Committee has six areas of responsibility: 1) agricultural production, 2) industry, 3) funds, 4) schools, 5) political education, and 6) the militia. It is also responsible for the maintenance of its central office. The commune RC decides on annual production plans with the advice of brigade and production team leaders and issues orders to the brigade RCs, who, in turn, make work allotments for the production teams. Implementation of the plans is insured by frequent inspections, the commune checking on the brigades and the brigades on the production units.

Unlike ordinary members of the commune, whose income is determined by their work points, the cadres are paid by the state and earn an average upper-middle salary of between 500 and 600 yuan per year. Currently, equipment is owned at all three organizational levels—production team, brigade, and commune. Liang predicts less ownership by the production team and brigade and more by the commune, an appropriate continuation of the trend toward greater socialization. He estimates this will take several decades through natural evolutionary process. Even now some equipment is financed through rentals to production units or brigades on requisition from a commune pool; for example, it costs 10 yuan to rent a tractor and a trained operator for one day. The future will see the extension of this practice.

Ideal communal life aspires to self-sufficiency. The six factories operated by the commune fit into this basic directive of socialization. The bricks and the lime manufactured in two commune factories are, of course, used directly for construction and fertilization. Other factories for construction and repair of farm tools, motors, and trucks maintain the meager number of machines. The sixth factory, called a "truck team," seemed to be a collection of mechanics and drivers whose job it was to keep the wheels rolling out on the field and the road when the trucks were not in need of factory maintenance.

Another basic communal ingredient is provided by the small stores in each production unit. We visited the four near the schools of our own production unit and found the merchandise limited and uninteresting. Nonetheless, easy access to such items as new socks, beer, tea, and sewing supplies obviously pleases the peasants.

If Lugou Ch'iao is at all typical of communes in China, and if an extrapolation from Lugou Ch'iao to communes in general were to be made, such statistics would show that the commune has become the instrument for the social betterment of about 600 million people—possibly the most revolutionary social instrumentality the world has known.

On another visit, Liang and the other leaders pridefully conducted us on a tour of their newest enterprise, a duck farm, operated by the Tai Ping Ch'iao, or Peaceful Bridge Brigade. It was started just one year ago, following an innovative decision by the commune Revolutionary Committee. Aware of the large demand for Peking ducks both in China and abroad and, encouraged by the progress of the commune in the last decade, the Committee turned to the new venture as a means of increased profit for the commune's capital fund. No one at Lugou Ch'iao was experienced in mass duck production, but, with the help of duck experts from a nearby commune, seven knowledgeable workers were gathered to start the operation.

The new unit has capacity for 18,000 eggs and 1,000 ducks. When we were there, 700 mature ducks were actually producing eggs, and 300 were almost at that stage. The farm maintains a ratio of one male for every four females, and the average female produces 190 eggs per year, mostly at night. We were told that about 82 percent of all the eggs are fertile and are used to produce young ducks; the infertile eggs are sold for eating.

Each duck sells for 5 yuan. The duck manure, 6 to 7 million *catties* of which are produced in this one unit, is extremely val-

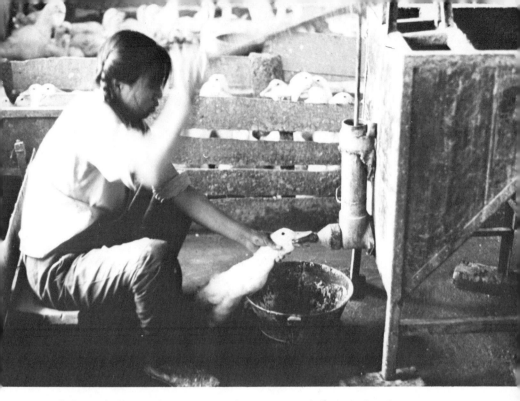

A balanced diet and rapid growth are assured by regular force feeding at Lugou Ch'iao's duck farm.

uable as it is considered the best of all manures for agriculture, even without further treatment. Feathers are another by-product —for fertilizer as well as down. Each month the ducks consume about 120,000 *catties* of grain obtained from the government, as well as other locally produced foods.

The eggs are hatched in an incubator, stabilized at 37.8° centigrade by fans in a heated enclosure. A new batch of eggs is started each week and requires twenty-eight days of incubation. Upon hatching, the young ducklings are force-fed a mash of corn, beancake, fish powder, *kaoliang,* and grass and only sixty days later are sent to market—mostly live—for export to Hong Kong. Others are killed, dressed, and frozen for shipment. For the transport of live ducks, special three-story air-conditioned railroad cars are used.

The force-feeding is not pretty, but it seems very efficient. The ducks are herded into an enclosure, which narrows progressively

The ducks go swimming twice on hot days as high temperatures are the worst enemy of successful production. The duck farm is a fairly new and profitable venture at Lugou Ch'iao.

until only one duck at a time can advance. At the apex sits a farm worker who grasps each duck in turn; he opens the duck's mouth, puts it around a rubber pipe attached to a hopper full of the mash, and then depresses a lever that forces the correct amount of feed down the duck's throat. Despite the unesthetic manner of feeding, the ducks thrive and grow rapidly. As there are apparently no important duck diseases, the main enemy to high productivity is the extreme heat. Because of this, the ducks are allowed to go swimming two times a day.

The peasants in the duck farm work nine hours within a twelve-hour shift. There are two shifts each day; since the ducks must be fed every six hours, workers alternate day and night shifts and receive a day of rest as the transition from one schedule to the other. All money from the sale of the ducks is returned to the brigade and distributed to the workers according to their merit work points. As usual, different workers earn different rewards.

The average salary is about 600 yuan per year; the workers told us that they can save about half of this, or enough to build one room of a house. Other favorite outlays for savings are sewing machines, costing 180 yuan, bicycles, at about 150 yuan, watches, from 80 to 120 yuan, and better clothing, furniture, and household utensils, all of which are becoming more readily available.

Our transportation to and from the duck farm provided another example of the subtlety and active-passive resistance of our Chinese hosts to the changes we wanted to introduce into their plans for us. We had made it perfectly clear in Peking that we did not enjoy riding around in limousines. Thus, the problem arose of how to transport us from our production unit to the duck farm, several miles away, on a very hot day. We were told that we could walk down the road half a kilometer, where we could catch a bus. We started off with Li, Liang, and Juo. The day was really beastly hot; obviously we were in for an uncomfortable time. Just then a truck "happened" down the road. Liang acted surprised and overjoyed. He signaled the driver, who drew to a stop. Oddly enough, the truck was headed toward the vicinity of the duck farm, and the driver graciously agreed to give us a lift. The tailgate was swung down, we all climbed up in back—except for Dale, who was given a seat in the cab—and off we went. To make the playacting look legitimate (or so it seemed to me), the truck stopped several hundred yards from the duck farm, and we did in fact walk the last dusty bit of our journey. We arrived, very hot and sweaty, to be greeted by three other members of the Revolutionary Committee, who were ready with freshly prepared wash basins, washcloths, soap, towels, and cups of tea.

When our visit to the duck farm was over, we expected to start back on foot, but this time there was not quite so much dissemblance. A small truck, built over a motorcycle, drew up, obviously for us. To our complete amazement, our hosts started to pile chairs in the back for us to sit on. We told them we would rather squat on the floor, which we did. In great triumph, clatter, and dust, we arrived back at our production unit. We had been driven, of course, in both directions deliberately and according to plan, and without limousines.

Unlike our trip to the duck farm, our firsthand experience with the medical services at Lugou Ch'iao was unplanned but equally educational. Dale was the first victim. Toward the end of our first week she developed aches and pains and a slight fever. She had decided to let the mild illness run its course, but it so happened that the next morning we were given a tour of the brigade clinic. A delegation of about six brigade leaders conducted us to a modest six-room building that housed facilities for all types of out-patient care as well as a few beds for temporary hospitalization. Newly whitewashed, spotlessly clean, it had the antiseptic air that makes you feel it is a very good place to be when you are unwell. The seven members of the medical staff (six women and one man) serve about 500 families or 2,100 people. All are "barefoot doctors," who have received between a few months' and one year's training in surgery, herbal medicine, and acupuncture and now work part time at the clinic and part time, barefoot, in the fields. The morning of our visit, two young women were ministering to half a dozen patients suffering from minor stomach upsets and headaches. One, with a sprained ankle, had received treatment of manipulation, binding, and medication. The doctors hastened to explain to us that of course serious illnesses, including broken bones, were referred to the commune hospital, to which truck ambulance transportation was available.

Dale turned to Li and asked him to mention her illness to one of the barefoot doctors on duty. The young woman attended her immediately with a bi f examination, discovered that she did in fact have a slight fever, a d recommended bed rest. Dale complied. That evening the same barefoot doctor appeared in our courtyard with herbal medicine, which was immediately brewed for Dale by Chang Shu-mei. Everyone around was intensely interested; they were sure the dosage would prove most unpleasant for Dale, and they brought tea to wash away the bad effects. But she found it only mildly bitter, enough to make it seem properly remedial, and promised to take it as prescribed every morning and evening for several days.

Our hosts must have felt that the services of a barefoot doctor, while sufficient for one of their own number, were not so for a visiting American. Therefore, on the second day of Dale's illness, a delegation of two medical doctors and two barefoot doctors came for further examination. It was begun by a traditional Chinese physician, a dignified man in his late forties with receding hair,

[112]

extremely high cheekbones, and a habit of throwing his head back so that he always looked as if he were addressing the sky. His procedure consisted of taking Dale's pulse in a variety of ways and in various locations. Then, after much thought while pacing back and forth, *he told her* that her symptoms were a heavy head, dry throat, and fever, that her stomach was upset, and that she had slept poorly the night before. He was right in almost every case, but of course Dale, had she been consulted, could have told him all this. After making several pronouncements about the importance of getting the inner fire into harmony with the outer body, he sat down, and the Western doctor took over.

She was a slender woman in her early thirties with modern medical training. Her procedure was more familiar: she took Dale's temperature (37.1° centigrade, a little above normal), examined her with a stethoscope, tongue depressor, and a flashlight beam in her eyes, then took her blood pressure (120 over 80, or normal). She asked Dale a few questions about how she felt and then deferred to the two young barefoot doctors, who proceeded with their own type of examination. Finally all four sat down together to confer about medicines and treatment. The recommendation was enforced bed rest for several days and the

The peasants at Lugou Ch'iao take great pride in their hospital, which they themselves constructed in 1971.

prescription of several medicines (both Western and Chinese), which eventually resulted in complete cure.

These four practitioners all came from the staff of the commune hospital, a modern two-story structure that, during our visit several days later, further confirmed our good opinions of medical care in China. It had been completed just about a year before through the labors of the commune workers themselves. It comprises about thirty-six beds and a staff (three-quarters women) of twelve regular doctors and twenty-five barefoot doctors who handle some two hundred cases a day. Its facilities include X-ray, operating rooms for all minor surgery, delivery rooms, and a laboratory for all standard medical tests. We saw microscopes, centrifuge, balances, sterilizers, and incubators, and of course, provision for ready referral and consultation in Peking. We talked to a young female internist, who had received five years of medical training—three and a half years of basic study at Wuhan University and one and a half years of clinical work. She was now attached to a Peking Hospital and on temporary duty at Lugou Ch'iao.

Beth subsequently suffered a lesser form of the same flulike illness, for which she received no medicine, but, along with Dale, the solicitous attention of all the members of the compound. She was urged to remain on her *k'ang,* and a special soup with eggs in it was supplied in great quantity. When we asked if we were not depleting their egg supply, our hosts reassured us that the chickens produced plenty of eggs. And besides, they had money enough to buy whatever extra was needed at the stores just a short distance from our compound. After a day of rest and all that good food, Beth shook off her illness and returned to work, though on a slightly reduced schedule.

We were overwhelmed and impressed by the kindness and efficiency of this medical care, as well as by the direct evidence that, in the short space of twenty-two years, China had completely transformed the health status of one-fourth of the world's people.

The transformation in educational standards too is evidenced at Lugou Ch'iao, and everyone is understandably proud of their schools. They represent an undeniable achievement, for parents, most of whom are still struggling to learn to read and write, are now assured that their children will master these skills at an early age. Before 1958 there were ten primary schools and no middle schools on the commune. Now there are nineteen primary schools and five middle schools. All children go to primary school from ages seven to twelve, then on to lower-middle school until age sixteen. About 20 percent of these students will attend upper-middle school until the age of eighteen, and then, after several years of productive labor on a commune, in a factory, or in the People's Liberation Army, they may be nominated for further study at a university.

We spent a morning at one of the primary schools run by our brigade. Because of the shortage of space for the five hundred students in grades one to six, classes are conducted in two shifts, the first from 8:00 to 11:45 A.M., the second from 2:00 to 5:45 P.M., with four classes per shift, each of which lasts about forty-five minutes. About forty students attend each class and are taught by different teachers in each subject.

The classrooms, small, concrete-floored, and undecorated, all feature large pictures of Chairman Mao on the wall in the front and his quotations on the blackboard in the back. Each contains wooden desks and chairs, arranged in rows by twos. Generally boys sit with boys and girls with girls. The teachers seemed quite authoritarian and the children strictly disciplined. When the teacher enters, the class stands up and then, at a signal, sits down as one body with military precision. Each time we entered a classroom, all the students rose and clapped in unison.

All pupils study Chinese language, mathematics, music, sports, drawing, and politics. In grade four they branch out into general knowledge and industrial knowledge, which, translated, means learning the skills of *laodung* in actual practice on the commune. School is in session from March to July, with a month's vacation in August, and from September to January, with a month's vacation in February—an arrangement surely planned to coordinate with the commune's agricultural production schedule.

The teaching staff numbers twenty-two, fifteen women and seven men. Three are villagers, and the others, from Peking, were appointed by the commune RC. Teachers are trained, upon completion of middle school and the mandatory work years that follow it, through three years of study in educational methods and their subject specialty. They are paid by the state about 50 yuan a month,

[115]

or about the same as the average peasant earns. No one is trained in special instruction, guidance, or psychology. We were told that children with special problems receive help from teachers or "mutual self-help" groups of their peers. Thus it appears that Dale's vocation as a psychologist-specialist in work with disturbed children simply does not exist in China. This of course surprised us all and greatly disappointed her.

In a fourth-grade mathematics class, students were learning to use the abacus. They recited in unison until three addition problems were put on the board: 300 plus 85 plus 35; 704 plus 106; 340 plus 637. Volunteers went to the front of the room, and their answers and manipulations of a large demonstration abacus were criticized by the class. The teacher wandered around the room while the students were working on the problem, offering help in a quiet, friendly way.

We went next to a sixth-grade language class where the teacher stood up in front and read loudly from a textbook. She then asked questions, complimenting each student when he recited loudly and sat down smartly. The purpose of this class was to teach reading, writing, grammar, and politics—or how to serve the people according to Mao's teachings. We asked to see the textbook, and Li explained its contents: the words of the Internationale, Chairman Mao's poems, stories about the miseries of life before Liberation and the great advances under the leadership of the Party and Chairman Mao as well as stories about Revolutionary martyrs and the people of Vietnam downing U.S. planes, two Chinese folktales, and several pages of grammar. The use of all texts, and the curriculum in general, is decided by the Peking Municipal Revolutionary Committee's education department, which has supervisory control over each local school's RC. Such a committee guides this elementary school. It has three members, two appointed from the Communist Party and one, a teacher, elected by the whole school community.

After school some students must attend organized homework sessions, and others, such as the Young Pioneers and Red Guards, engage in more special activities—visiting the tombs of Revolutionary heroes or talking to old peasant families to learn about the class struggle. Members of these groups generally number over 50 percent of the student body. They are elected by teachers and

The playground of a lower-middle school at Lugou Ch'iao. The rows of concrete tables evidence the popularity of table tennis. In the picture below, a championship match is being held between the leading players of two classes. Various school buildings are in the background.

fellow students on the basis of moral, political, physical, and intellectual worthiness.

On a subsequent day we visited the brigade lower-middle school, which has about one thousand students between the ages of twelve and sixteen, forty-three teachers (only 40 percent female), ten staff members, and instruction in twenty different subjects. This school was founded in 1968, and its curriculum is planned especially for the needs of the commune families. The new building is a simple two-story structure, well maintained, and attractively landscaped.

We first visited a chemistry class for third-year students. Forty-eight students crowded into this classroom, but they were all eager and interested, and the teacher had unusually effective control. A young woman of very great talent, she was delivering a lecture about liquids, solids, and solutions. She skillfully demonstrated the basic principles of her subject with chemicals, test tubes, and a Bunsen burner. She had the students' rapt attention and conducted what would have been a highly successful lesson in any school system.

Our visit to an English-language class produced a very different impression. The young male teacher, mechanical and unsure of himself, asked for volunteers to read new words. After each student read, he delivered the same comment, "Thank you, sit down." Was he so inhibited because of the presence of English-speaking visitors? We could not tell, but it was stultifying, and we could not leave soon enough. We did manage to look at the books in English these fifteen-year-olds were reading and again found them propagandistic with chapter titles like: "The World's People Love Chairman Mao," "The African People Love Chairman Mao," and so on. The exercise book contained written and oral drills on similar themes.

The courses taught in this lower-middle school include history of China, Chinese literature, mathematics, politics, agriculture, physics, chemistry, geography, foreign languages, music, physical training, painting, and drawing. Among the foreign languages, English is the most widely taught, with seventeen classes to three for Russian. An interesting adjunct to regular study is a shop in which students work three weeks each term manufacturing acupuncture needles.

[118]

About 20 percent of each class will advance to upper-middle school, while 40 percent go to work in factories, and the other 40 percent to communes. In order to be accepted in senior-middle school, students must take an examination but, as we were repeatedly told, not a competitive examination. To a Westerner this seems a contradiction in terms. Apparently, however, students make the first selection of candidates, who are then screened by the teachers, and finally approved by the RC. In the selection process attitude, politics, and morale are as important as scholarly competence.

The Revolutionary Committee for this school now has nine members, who were first nominated by the masses and then, after discussion, approved by the Communist Party committee. Although six members are teachers, clearly the Communist Party, as well as the commune RC, have considerable authority over curriculum and other activities.

A tremendously active sports program enlivened the large field outside the school. Young people were participating eagerly in basketball, volleyball, Ping-Pong, and gymnastics. In the courtyard alongside rows of concrete Ping-Pong tables, students arranged chairs for a match. Boys play against boys and girls against girls. We witnessed a basketball game between two classes. Before play started, the teams lined up facing each other and recited a sportsman's credo, which emphasized the importance of clean play and good competition over winning. The players of the opposing teams then shook hands and, after the tip-off by the two centers, played vigorously and skillfully. Dribbling was a bit erratic, however, because of the uneven surface of the court.

Overall, our reactions to the schools were mixed. On the positive side is the universal availability of basic education up to age sixteen for all children, irrespective of background or economic status. The schools are decent places where students learn to socialize well, and the teachers are dedicated and well trained. But the propagandistic nature and rigidity of much of the curriculum disturbed us and made us question whether these young minds were being trained for inquiry or molded into a single line of thought.

Except for the sports programs at the schools, entertainment and relaxation seemed exceedingly sparse at Lugou Ch'iao. One

At the beginning of a spirited basketball game between two classes of the lower-middle school, the opposing players lined up, recited a sportsman's creed emphasizing the value of competition over winning, then shook hands before the tip-off.

day, however, a mobile movie team arrived to present a color film of the Revolutionary ballet, "The White-Haired Girl," especially for our production team. I had seen this production in Shanghai the year before in the princely company of Norodom Sihanouk of Cambodia, but the change in surroundings even heightened my interest. The showing was to take place that evening in the central production team courtyard. A large sheet was stoutly secured to a building by an arrangement of ropes and the projector set up across the courtyard in the granary. Peasants arrived in the darkness carrying stools, which they lined up in theaterlike rows. Many of them had seen it before, but all were enthusiastic. They followed the melodramatic plot intently, frequently humming and singing along with the familiar music, much of which we had heard during rest periods in the rice paddies.

It was a gusty evening, and the sheet screen danced in the wind. About three-quarters of the movie had been shown when a tremendous thunderclap and the beginnings of a rainstorm caused a temporary postponement, and then a cancellation, of the rest of the performance. Despite this disappointment, the audience had obviously greatly appreciated this break in the routine of almost endless work.

In our position as guests we did manage to punctuate this routine with some special festivities. Since our thirty-first wedding anniversary fell on June 27, 1972, we decided to make it an occasion for giving our hosts a party. On the preceding day I was scheduled to make a trip into Peking to visit Tsinghua University, at which time I planned to pick up such delicacies as cakes, candies, and liquor. We then told Shih and the two Changs (Lao and Syao) our plans—that in our country it was the custom for people who were marking an anniversary to give a party for their friends. They listened politely, and we thought they understood and agreed, but we learned very soon that they would give the party for us and would not permit the reverse.

On the appointed day there was great activity. Mounds of string beans were brought in from the garden, for we were to feast on *chiao-tse,* the tiny dumpling delicacy beloved of all who admire Chinese cuisine. The beans were spread on boards for chopping, and soon all were caught up joyfully in the communal effort. Chang Shu-mei was kneading a great mass of dough so resistant that she

Preparations for our anniversary feast. Above, rounds of dough are cut and rolled for the delectable steamed dumpling chiao-tse, and below, green beans are painstakingly cut lengthwise with a scissors before marination in a soy bean sauce. In the background are the stoves in the cook shed.

had to exert extreme physical pressure. I offered to help and ultimately did with a sort of karate-chop technique. She burst into giggles. When the dough was ready, it was shaped into a long snakelike tube, from which small circles were sliced. These were dextrously rolled out into dumpling shells with a tiny rolling pin, whirled with magical speed by the mother of the renter family. The shells were divided among various tables around which others were seated ready to fill them.

The stuffing had a complex recipe, starting with the chopping of the string beans. After the beans could be no more finely minced, the entire mass was put between layers of coarse cloth and twisted to rid it of all excess juice. The resultant mush was then mixed with finely chopped, cooked lamb, properly seasoned with herbs and spices, and stuffed into the dough shells to form the dumplings. The ordinary way to seal the *chiao-tse* was simply to fold it in half and crimp it, producing a pocket-shaped semicircle. As in most endeavors, artistry can lend enhancement. In this case, the virtuoso was Old Shih himself, whose fingers flew over the dough, pleating it into the shape of a perfect grain of wheat. Beth was intrigued, and Shih patiently helped her learn how to form the distinctive little dumplings.

As we finished the *chiao-tse,* we placed them on circular trays made of finely woven bamboo. These trays were taken to the cooking shed, where they were placed in layers three or four deep in a large pot, and steamed for fifteen or twenty minutes. By that time we were all ready and waiting to relish them. It was a universal treat, accompanied by lots of beer, bought at a local store and cooled in buckets full of cold well water. There were also the usual fresh vegetables, including especially giant beefsteak tomatoes, sliced coarsely and coated with sugar. Toward the end of the meal other liquors were served—a sweet red grape wine, a fiery liquor made from the seeds of *kaoliang* grass, somewhat similar to Swedish akvavit, and finally a bottle of cognac we had brought from Paris.

The anniversary feast generated many good feelings—much hilarity, backslapping, joke telling, and singing—and was a truly festive evening. Li told us later that Lao Chang had become so stimulated by all this activity he had been virtually unable to sleep. He had awakened very early, still exhilarated and excited, and had taken half a day to calm down.

One afternoon in the courtyard, Beth and I started quietly tossing a frisbee, one of the small plastic disks so popular in America. With a flick of the wrist, they can be made to float long and short distances, curving up, down, and sideways, and are the basis of several games. Before long all the children had gathered around—and not just to watch. They wanted to learn to play. So every day thereafter included a frisbee session. When we left the commune the frisbee stayed behind—perhaps starting a new kind of Cultural Revolution of their own, one that includes more simple games and music of the kind we had enjoyed with our friends and more genuine leisure and fun, an aspect of life too often neglected in the rigid routine demanded by the crusade for ever-higher production.

After about two weeks on the commune we realized that, given our inability to speak more effectively with our friends than our limited knowledge of their language allowed, we had seen and experienced all that was possible at Lugou Ch'iao and would learn little by extending our stay. It was time to see other aspects of life in China. We therefore informed our hosts in Peking that we would like to leave quite soon. Dale and Beth were planning to visit the great ceramics center at T'ang-shan, and I would return to Shanghai to talk at length with my friends in the scientific and agricultural institutions there.

No sooner had this news spread in the commune than we were again visited by Liang and the other commune and brigade officials, who said they would like to give us a farewell party. They invited us to the commune headquarters, where we could be appropriately feted. We explained to them that our allegiance and emotional attachment were mainly to the family in our compound. Couldn't they arrange to hold the party there? We recognized that this might cause additional work and disruption of the routine for our hardworking friends, but we knew that they and we would appreciate that sort of farewell. After some consultation, those arrangements were made.

The preparations for the party were hectic. Everyone pitched in, as once again we furnished the excuse for laying aside worldly cares and duties in order to attend to sheer pleasure. Mounds of *chiao-tse* were made. Fresh vegetables of all kinds were gathered, carefully washed, sliced, and esthetically arranged on plates. Delicious small watermelons, newly ripe, were an addition to the menu. Much beer, wine, and *kaoliang* were purchased and cooled. Most impressive, the normal dining procedure was completely revamped. Knowing that we preferred to eat as a group around one table rather than separately and alone first, our hosts constructed their version of a banquet table. Two high tables, in addition to our usual dining table, were placed in a direct line with the door of the old folks' house. The door was propped open and out into the courtyard the banquet table continued with a line of smaller tables. When we came together for the feast, we were all seated at the same table and at the same time, even the small children. Of course Chang Shu-mei and several older grandchildren were busy scurrying around making our meal generally pleasant and overflowing with food, warmth, and hospitality. The commune and brigade officials with whom we had had closest contact also attended, an interesting compromise between Western informality and Chinese protocol. There were a few toasts, a few *kambeis* to international amity and to individual friendship, but for the most part we sat eating, talking loudly, singing a few songs, and acting

Our friends at Lugou Ch'iao gave us a farewell banquet as heartwarming as it was bountiful.

like good friends who were about to say goodbye. When the last piece of watermelon had been consumed at the end of a long and lavish banquet, we all felt stuffed, happy, and a little sad that our adventure on the commune was coming to an end.

It was a remarkable moment; we really did not know these people well; we had never talked deeply; certainly interpreted conversations, fine for fact, leave much to be desired in the world of ideas. Yet we had worked, eaten, relaxed, and lived together as a family for two weeks. The rhythm of our lives had been caught up in the pace of commune activity. It was not surprising that both our hosts and we were a bit tearful when the final goodbyes were said. Dale embraced Old Shih, his wife, and a few children, but otherwise there was no outward display of emotion. Yet, as we clasped hands with each of our hosts and friends, looked them in the eye, and said "thank you and goodbye," we felt an emotional impact that only good friends experience at parting. Our feelings rather astounded us, because, with such vastly different cultures and life experiences, we had not thought we had enough in common to be so affected. But when they said, "Please come back again," we replied, "We will," and we both meant it.

Pride in their accomplishment radiates from the faces of the chairman and vice-chairman of the Beijing Yuetan's Revolutionary Committee who hold their factory's former product, a simple scales, as they stand in front of the present product, a complicated electronic muffle furnace.

7

New China's New Cities

ALTHOUGH ABOUT 80 percent of China's 800 million people live in the countryside, urban density in the eastern half of the country is high. Sixteen cities each embrace more than a million population, compared to six in the United States. With about 10 million within its municipal boundaries, Shanghai is now considered the world's largest city. Situated near the mouth of the Yangtze River, this teeming industrial conglomerate receives and distributes all the agricultural richness of the river's western plains, and, as China's most important seaport, it still serves as doorway to the rest of the world. Like New York, it is the commercial hub at the center of the east coast. Peking's more formal setting, with gracious parks, avenues, and public buildings, Washington-like, reflects its position of seven hundred years as the government center. Non-Mandarin-speaking Canton, in cultural and geographical isolation from the Han centers of the north, turns toward Indochina, a subtropical, Los Angeles sprawl on the South China Sea. The diversity of the cities is abundant and clearcut, but the samenesses, overlaid by the political might of the New China, impress the Westerner more forcefully.

For an American used to the problems and hectic pace of our highly developed urban centers, the most striking characteristics of these cities are orderliness and cleanliness, the sense of well-being and hope, and freedom from crime and strife. Everywhere the people go about their business patiently, purposefully, confidently, and courteously; they seem well fed, vigorous, and frequently exuberant; the skin sores, rashes, emaciation, and other physical deformities, so widespread in China before 1949, are now virtually absent. Gone too are the masses of beggars known to have dominated city streets in pre-Revolution days. Today laughter and jaunty behavior typify the groups, especially of young people, walking in the unlittered streets. Street cleaners, both men and women, abound, attacking the litter almost before it is tossed to the ground. Their efforts are greatly abetted, however, by the attitude of respect for their surroundings prevalent among the Chinese.

Law and order, as well, are maintained more by the prevailing high moral code than by the threat of police action. Armed policemen are nowhere to be seen in the streets; the officers on patrol duty seem to have little to do beyond direct traffic at the busiest intersections. In the neighborhoods, marshals and guards are usually residents—sometimes little old ladies—who help schoolchildren across streets and remind people of their civic duties.

While most Chinese cities are very crowded, they seem unhurried, almost leisurely in pace, compared to their American counterparts. They are also less varied in interest, less colorful, less

Even in Shanghai, city streets retain an air of tranquility despite extreme crowding. Trees are never far away. Pedestrians and bicyclists abound, but motorized vehicles are few.

exciting. Undoubtedly much of this derives from the scarcity of motorized traffic. There are no private motor vehicles at all, and as far as we could tell, the government has no plans as yet for changing this regulation. Buses, trucks, and cars are all owned by the government and used only for officially designated purposes like the transporting of foreigners, government business, shipment of market goods, and industrial needs. Because of the dearth of automobiles, atmospheric pollution does not yet pose the danger already apparent in many American cities, but the existing cars pollute as effectively as motor vehicles anywhere.

Bicycles of course are everywhere; they dominate the traffic. Peking's 3 to 4 million inhabitants own 1½ million. In all the cities we saw large bicycle parking lots located near most factories and public buildings. Many of the bicycles are actually tricycle style with good-sized carriers behind for passengers or parcels, and they give a meandering, disorderly character to the traffic flow. Bicyclists are obliged to keep to the right in the slow lanes, the faster ones veering to the left in order to pass. Needless to say, different bicyclists proceed at different rates of speed, and the result is passers of the passers and a continuous leftward encroachment on the remaining free road space. When a car, bus, or truck wants to penetrate the forest of bicycles, the accepted practice in getting them to move aside is liberal use of the horn. And in general, the peace in city streets does not imply quiet, as honking is a significant component of life in all of China's cities.

Good public transportation is also available for workers in the form of electric trolley buses and some diesel buses. These bus lines crisscross the major thoroughfares in all the cities we visited. Toward the end of our 1972 visit we had occasion to use the buses several times. In many ways it was just like riding a bus in a big city anywhere, but there were important differences. The buses appear every few minutes, and although they are crowded, and therefore somewhat uncomfortable, seats always mysteriously appeared for us. This embarrassed us, but we accepted it, recognizing that such politeness and deference toward foreigners remain essentials of Chinese culture. Courtesy and consideration extended beyond their treatment of us, however: riders waited their turn and never violated line order, and the drivers operated with cognizance of the needs of pedestrians and passengers alike. The cost

Bicycles are everywhere. In the Peking parking lot above, an attendant charges a small fee to park bicycles and keep them till the owner's return. Below, bicycles have been left unlocked in front of a news bulletin board at a Hangchou factory.

is enviable by American standards—.05 yuan (U.S. $.02) or less to go anywhere in the city. Few children were in evidence on the buses, and those we saw were always accompanied by adults, never alone. Everyone is laden with bags and parcels, but no one eats and no one reads.

In Peking a subway, years in the building, at present extends that city's public transportation system fifteen miles into the western suburbs, and construction is underway to continue the line in a loop twelve miles long through the northern suburbs. Though not widely used as yet, it is a model of planning for future needs, providing not only transportation but also an underground bomb shelter. After the 1969 Soviet-Chinese confrontation at the Amur and Ussuri rivers on the northern border, the Chinese, fearful of a preemptive nuclear strike by the Russians, began construction of underground cities in metropolitan areas to protect their populations. As is the Chinese way with most necessary undertakings, this has been accomplished quietly and deliberately, even though it has dislocated urban life considerably.

Most Chinese cities comprise many separate, independent neighborhoods, each clustered around a factory or other center of production or commerce. Close by the factory, often surrounding it, are the apartment houses where the workers live; ringing these in turn are parks, theaters, and outdoor amusement arenas. Scattered throughout the community thus formed are hospitals, schools, markets, and a factory canteen. Such arrangements are being steadily developed and enhanced by carefully planned construction of whole new enclaves of factories, housing, and public buildings, especially in Peking, although a rooftop view of Canton revealed many such groups on the outskirts of that city. In more congested cities, like Shanghai, new workers' housing is beginning to appear, mainly at the periphery, but sometimes a city block is razed to locate a factory in the center of an existing older neighborhood. The proximity of housing to factory means that workers rarely need to allow for a long trip to and from their jobs but can get there easily on foot or bicycle or by a short bus ride. This is especially important for the numerous working mothers who must take young children to the factory crèche, nursery, or kindergarten before reporting for work.

The self-sufficiency of each neighborhood creates an environ-

Shanghai in the rain from the top of a nearby restaurant. This teeming commercial city has become the world's largest with the newest population figures of 10,820,000.

ment in which urban dwellers develop familiarity with, and attachment to, a particular district of their city rather than to the city as a whole; in this respect they may be as provincial as country dwellers. They can and do go to the center of their city for athletic events and other amusements, but this seems much more the exception than the rule. The need or the opportunity to travel between cities rarely arises and is actually not possible without special visas.

The Chinese take great pride in their developing industry and accordingly gave us many opportunities to visit factories. Although production details differ from one to another, all have many practices in common, which are well illustrated by Beijing Yuetan, the Number 1 Semiconductor Equipment Factory of the western district of Peking. The name of this factory is stamped on my memory, just as its trademark, Beijing Yuetan, is stamped everywhere in sight on its premises. It seemed such an un-Chinese word —until I recognized "Beijing" as the phoneticized version of Peking. Prior to the Cultural Revolution, this factory made one simple object, a scale for itinerant peddlers. This consisted of a rod to which were attached a pan and weights to achieve the balance. Today the factory employs 350 workers who manufacture high-precision, automatically controlled diffusion furnaces, the basic equipment for making electronic parts.

Originally only a hundred neighborhood housewives were employed, and they worked in a simple shed, but since 1965 the shed has become a series of good-looking modern buildings. Clean, quiet, and airy, they provide a relaxing place in which to work, free from the pressures of a larger installation. None of the original workers had more than a seventh-grade education, but, with the help of plans and advice from the professionals of nearby Tsinghua University, they have transformed their primitive operation with its two small machines into a busy, varied, and sophisticated center of productivity.

How did this all come about? The basic technique was the creation of a committee for innovation that brought together the most able workers in the factory. This group, freed from normal work requirements, was mandated to prepare a plan for diversification of the factory and for its entrée into more complex techniques. The innovative personnel at Number 1 Semiconductor Equipment included seven untrained housewives, one middle-school student, an accountant, an experienced factory worker, and a worker on loan from another factory. While this group did its research and produced plans for new production schemes, the remaining workers vowed to work harder so that production would not decline. We observed the use of this same model for upgrading and change in many enterprises—from farm, to factory, to hospital.

The university experts suggested several plans, which the workers tried to implement with disastrous results. One worker couldn't read blueprints, several got sick from studying too hard, others did not have the manual dexterity to perform the tasks required. But they persevered, began production haltingly, and by constant correction of errors mastered the new technology within three months.

All of this took place in 1965–66 during the fierce struggle between the political lines advocated by Mao Tse-tung and Liu Shao-ch'i, the latter at that time still head of state. In general, we were told, those following Liu were more conservative, even pessimistic. They argued that much more elaborate laboratories, including marble floors, temperature control, improved cleanliness, and more sophisticated tools, were needed before they could hope to produce semiconductors efficiently. The head engineer, a supporter of Liu, spent some 10,000 yuan in various experiments that came to naught. Finally the workers, following Chairman Mao's advice, "Dare to Think, Dare to Act," deposed their superior and took over the planning themselves. After an additional seven months they succeeded in organizing the factory rationally.

Beijing Yuetan diffusion furnaces are now shipped to electronics factories throughout mainland China. The factory's efforts have helped China gain self-sufficiency in the production of such furnaces, all of which had previously been imported. The workers told us with pride that models of their product were displayed at the Canton Trade Fair in 1970. Their output has gone up constantly; their quotas were overfulfilled by 12 percent in 1969, four months ahead of schedule, and were 2½ times that of 1968. In 1970 they again achieved a production increase of 2½ times, 110 days ahead of schedule.

Now they aim to improve the quality of their product. For example, they plan to substitute transistors for the vacuum tubes currently employed. This suggestion was made by two young workers who had come to the factory in 1966 at the age of seventeen. The workers all firmly asserted that the teachings of Chairman Mao had strengthened their confidence and thus their ability to innovate. The university scientists who had originally advised the workers came to visit the plant, recognized the high quality of their product, and adopted it, as well as the new production techniques, as models for classroom study.

As the workers' capabilities expanded, so did their boldness toward innovation. They used to buy a complex machine from the U.S.S.R. at a cost of 25,000 to 30,000 yuan; their own models, now being manufactured in the plant, cost them only 6,000 to

8,500 yuan. They copied a piece of Japanese equipment from a pattern obtained in 1969 and now produce it more cheaply than they can buy it. A new high-frequency oven used to cost them 300,000 yuan, but their own product costs 50,000 yuan. A miniaturized oven, weighing only 7½ kilograms, has replaced an older 134-kilogram machine.

Like all successful factories of modest size, Beijing Yuetan is entitled to one piece of new equipment from the state each year. But in some instances, because of their newly found self-reliance, the workers have preferred to buy old equipment and renovate it. Whenever they want to alter production plans drastically, they must first get the approval of the Revolutionary Committee of the west district of Peking. Their reputation is so good they have almost never been refused permission to do as they wanted. They emphasized that this has been accomplished in a factory in which 70 percent of the workers are relatively unskilled women. The deputy chairman and six of the nine Revolutionary Committee members are women—a remarkable transformation in a country where many women still suffer the bound feet of the era before 1949.

At a machine-tools factory in Shanghai women work as lathe operators.

As in most Chinese factories the work schedule calls for six days of labor a week, eight hours a day—from 8:00 to 12:00 and 2:00 to 6:00. Mothers of very young children usually get some time off each day to visit the nursery. Days off in all forms of urban employment are staggered so that all factories and shops operate all day, every day. Services are therefore available on everyone's days off, and the shops and streets handle a uniform, but constantly changing, flow of people. We were assured that family members are in general able to arrange the same weekly days off.

The average salary at Beijing Yuetan of 35½ yuan per month is low by standards of other factories, which average as high as 50 to 60 yuan per month. Individual salaries differ somewhat, depending on length of service, skill, and political consciousness but not on number of children. Services at the factory include a day nursery, a canteen, a clinic with paramedical personnel on duty, and occasional free entertainment. Paid vacations are not a regular feature of the work arrangements, and it appears that only those persons whose homes are far away or who are separated from their families receive fifteen-day paid vacations; the other workers do not know the meaning of a rest away from work. They do, however, retire relatively early, men at 60 and women at 55. In general, they receive about half of their maximum monthly pay as a pension, and up to 70 percent for exceptionally long service.

Job requirements tend to segregate men and women at Beijing Yuetan, as in most factories we visited, the women performing more painstaking, sedentary assembly jobs, while the men do the heavier, more active work. At a large knitting mill, I noticed that the troubleshooters, who monitored the long rows of machines, were always older women; age, too, divides workers into particular kinds of jobs. In all factories the work demanding less skill is handled by younger people.

Supervision at Beijing Yuetan is in the hands of the Revolutionary Committee elected by the workers. In addition, the factory has an active branch of the Communist Party. Its thirty-two members provide unified leadership for the RC, seven of whose nine members belong to the Party. The guidelines of the "three-in-one principle" are followed: the worker members of the RC concern-

All Chinese value physical fitness. A rest break gives these handi-craft workers an opportunity to exercise—through dance routines in the factory courtyard.

ing themselves mainly with administrative affairs and production details while the Party members on the committee hammer out the broad ideological framework for operation of the factory and the coordination of its enterprise with the overall plans for the region. This adds up to a mechanism for insuring that the factory "puts politics in command."

RC members are elected by the workers after nomination of a slate at mass meetings. The terms of office are unstipulated, but all current members have served uninterruptedly since 1968. Any seriously incompetent RC member could be removed and replaced in a new election. The workers described matter-of-factly the one instance at Beijing Yuetan when an elected RC member was not approved by higher authorities. The reasons given were political. After these were stated and discussed openly, an alternate was elected, and the workers all accepted equably the revision of their original decision.

The atmosphere during our tour of Beijing Yuetan, and indeed

China's ancient crafts are carefully preserved today in the New China's handicraft factories. Here a master craftsman delicately chisels ivory into an elaborate design, following the pattern set up on the shelf before him.

all factory tours, was cordial, though rather self-conscious, as we were always accompanied by a large delegation of RC members. Workers applauded as we entered each room; most of them smiled broadly and continuously, posed proudly for our picture-taking, and seemed delighted that visitors could observe firsthand the great progress made by ordinary Chinese people. Even the children in the nursery applauded us, and their comments were translated to us as happiness at seeing friendly Americans.

In Shanghai, Hangchou, and Peking we visited China's renowned handicraft factories, where traditional artisanship supplanted the new technology as the most conspicuous feature. We saw skilled craftsmen with fine power-driven tools and hand implements shape large pieces of ivory into incredibly intricate landscapes and tableaus. Other groups carved exquisite animal shapes, hanging bowls, figurines, and jewelry out of jade with the exacting technique and hand-powered drilling required by that brittle substance. Delicate paint brushes are used to decorate duck eggs, and peculiar curved brushes, to paint the insides of tiny bottles; both art forms were strange to us but traditional in China. Extreme patience must be the chief attribute of the artisans who work in cloisonné. The base is a carefully shaped copper bowl or vase on which small copper strips are arranged in the outline of an intricate design. The depressions in the minute spaces between the stripping are then laboriously filled with pigment, and fired, refilled, and refired until the surface is smooth, and finally the whole is polished to yield the richly colored patterns characteristic of cloisonné ware. In a variation of this technique, repeated layers of a spongy lacquer are applied to the copper vases and bowls. After a diagram is drawn on the lacquer, it is carefully dissected with sharp tools, yielding an art object not only geometrically pleasing but very sturdy.

In most cases we observed handicrafts in small specialized factories like the silk-weaving mill in Hangchou. Production at the huge arts and crafts factory in Peking, however, comprises eleven traditional skills and employs 1,030 workers, 40 percent of whom are women. It is probably the only such comprehensive factory in China.

A particular disappointment for us was the discovery that pottery is not included in the ranks of prized handicrafts. When my

A cloisonné craftsman polishes a large copper vase to prepare it for decorating.

Silk is woven by modern methods at a Hangchou textile mill. The punch cards (left) are coded for the design, and when they are run through the machine, woven pictures (like the one of Chou En-lai below) are mass produced.

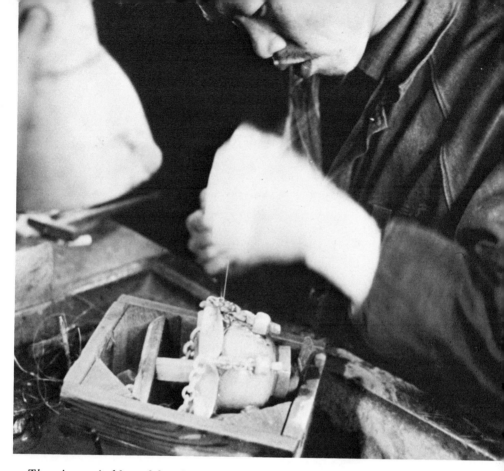

The picture is blurred by the movement of this man's hand. The operation involves a small bowlike instrument, the string of which has been wound around a tiny drill so that when he saws deftly and rapidly with the bow, the drill whirls in the jade. Graceful pots and chains like these are carved entirely from one piece of jade, a substance so brittle only hand tools can be used.

daughter Beth visited T'ang-shan, the pottery center southeast of Peking, she found that the emphasis was on mass production of designs of the "socialist-realist" type intended for everyday use. Esthetic considerations do not dominate, as in the other crafts, the products of which are intended chiefly for export. Apparently China's traditional preeminence in the ceramic craft resides today in her museums of ancient treasures.

New artisans are trained in an apprentice-master system. The young study the craft with older master workers, doing the bidding of their mentors and learning by watching and emulating. In the jade-carving factory, the youthful apprentices sitting beside their seventy-year-old masters left an unforgettably endearing image in my mind. We were told that such older, skilled artisans, on nearing retirement, are allowed to choose their youthful successors. The Peking factory had just taken on two hundred such apprentices directly from middle school. Their formal training will last for three years, but it will be seven or eight years before they achieve real mastery of their various crafts. Apprentices receive about 20 yuan per month, the average wage is 60 yuan, and some highly skilled masters earn up to 140 yuan a month.

In all the handicraft factories, unlike other kinds of factories, men and women work side by side at all kinds of tasks. We were impressed by the subordinate role of these artisans as artists. In the screen-painting section of the Peking factory, for instance, we witnessed a design conference in progress. A black-and-white drawing of a plan for the separate panels of a standing screen had been mounted on the wall. All the workers of the group were gathered to criticize and ultimately to accept the design as it was. The artistic talents of these superb craftsmen seem to be used rarely or never to create individual designs or techniques. They are employed solely to copy from models predetermined by the factory Revolutionary Committees, whose decisions are final and derive as much from political as esthetic considerations.

An important aspect of life for factory workers throughout China is their continuing political education. In most cases it is organized by cadre or Communist Party representatives on the RC. The schedule for these thought-study sessions at Hangchou Number 6 Textile Mill typifies the arrangement in most other factories. The sessions are held after hours, three times a week for one and a half hours each time. The study groups number ten to twelve persons, and attendance is compulsory. Discussions include such varied subjects as job techniques, general culture, and news items—domestic and international. All these subjects are somehow blended with the application and examination of Mao's thoughts and the writings of Marx, Engels, Lenin, and Stalin, all of whom are also studied as subjects in their own right.

Many new Chinese factories have been built in quiet, gardenlike surroundings. The small, one- or two-storied red brick structures

Rugs are woven by traditional methods. The patterns are worked in the colored wool from the spindles (right), then tamped into place as below.

Many Chinese factories are set in gardenlike surroundings. This pleasantly landscaped walk connects two buildings at Hangchou's silk factory.

are of functional architecture with no hint of traditional Oriental design and are connected by tree-lined walks with copious green plantings, rock gardens, and flowers but rarely grass. Such a setting is no doubt less efficient than mammoth, highly rationalized production units, but the Chinese claim it fosters high morale and low boredom. Certain Western countries like Sweden, with advanced technologized production systems, have recently declared a similar interest in the effect of this decentralization and freedom from assembly-line repetitiousness on worker morale. The decentralized nature of Chinese production affords, in addition, protection against natural or military disasters. The production of any one item in China simply cannot be wiped out by an earthquake, or flood, or bombing at one major factory. Through this dispersal (and extensive underground shelters), the Chinese have achieved not only a reasonably efficient but also a safe and satisfactory environment in which workers can improve their skills and their productivity.

On the day of our visit to Beijing Yuetan, we chanced, on leaving the factory, to pass a large bustling market. Although a visit here had not been planned, we asked our guides to stop. Permission was immediately granted, and we wandered for an hour or more, observing both the products and the people buying them.

There are six such markets in Peking, attractive, airy, open, and fairly simple stores on main thoroughfares. Food of all kinds seemed abundant and not expensive, but on that day, everyone was most interested in the vegetables and fruit at their seasonal peak as well as in a big shipment of fresh fish. When we remarked on the long lines of people waiting to be served, we were told this was because we were visiting at the peak rush hour. There were also many smaller markets, street peddlers, and open fruit stands nearby, which were serving the needs of many people with no waiting.

Prices were posted for most items, usually in Chinese numerals, but occasionally in Arabic. No signs urged us to "Drink Coca-Cola" but plenty exhorted us to "Learn from Tachai" or "Dare to Think, Dare to Act." We noted the prices of certain staples: a dozen eggs, .90 yuan; a bar of soap, .37 to .40 yuan; wine, 1.1 to 4 yuan; brandy, 2.8 yuan; various prepared food dishes, .30 yuan.

Vegetables today are more abundant and cheaper in the cities than formerly because of improvements in distribution and marketing procedures fostered by communal organization. Planning by the Peking Municipal RC, for instance, includes produce quotas from Lugou Ch'iao especially for the Peking markets. So the midsummer market price for cucumbers was .38 yuan a pound and for radishes, .06 yuan. Tomatoes were .48 yuan a pound, but their season was only beginning, and the price was expected to drop to .03 yuan or less. Beef cost .70 yuan a pound; mutton, .60; pork, .80; fish, .40; and fish plus roe from the Amur River in the far north, 1.60. Rice costs about .18 yuan a pound; this price has been stable since 1949, the year of Liberation. Other prices vary somewhat, but fluctuations are due solely to seasonal considerations, not to speculation. Some commodities seemed costly; tea, for example, was 3 to 5 yuan per pound; jasmine tea, 4 to 7 yuan; and black tea, 9 yuan per pound, all to be managed on wages of 35 to 60 yuan per month. Always, however, price comparisons must be considered in the light of the absence of income and sales tax, the spending potential of several salaries in every family, rent, including all utilities, of 3 to 4 yuan per month, and practically free education and medical care for all.

The shoppers in the Peking market included about equal numbers of men and women, all in their loose-cut, workaday pants and shirts, mainly white, not tucked in. Marketing is obviously a serious proposition, for children neither accompanied their parents nor handled the shopping for them, even though the apartments where these people lived were all located within a few blocks.

On several occasions I had the opportunity to visit such living quarters, those of workers and of professional friends as well, in the apartment houses that cluster around factories, schools, and research institutes. Of functional architecture and red brick construction similar to the factories, the buildings are generally six elevatorless stories high with four apartments at each landing. Some have balconies that overlook the pleasantly landscaped gardens below. By American standards the living conditions would be considered quite crowded, although less so than in many sections of our largest cities. The accommodations are simple, but the

The area around city dwellers' apartments is pleasantly landscaped. Above, the apartments near number three knitting mill in Peking and, below, other apartments with outside balconies overlooking the garden. The buildings are rarely over six stories high, an effective curb on extreme population density.

people display the value they set on their improved conditions by the care they expend in keeping them orderly and very clean. Typically, an apartment for a family of four or five consists of two large rooms, perhaps sixteen by twenty feet each, plus a foyer, off of which are located a small kitchen and bathroom. Usually one room is used by the adults and the other by the children. In each of these rooms are found the beds (generally a double bed in the parents' room and several single beds arranged along the walls of the children's room) plus whatever other furniture the family possesses—chests of drawers, tables and chairs, some easy chairs, and, occasionally, bookcases. Most families own several art objects, such as porcelain vases and paintings, in addition to the inevitable portrait of Chairman Mao and at least one framed photograph of a historical spot in China, like Yenan.

Although the kitchens are primitive, family meal preparation is certainly possible. Cooking is done over a two-burner stove with coal or charcoal as the fuel. All the kitchens we saw had running cold water, and most of them had hot-water heaters as well, though without automatic controls. Refrigerators are rare. The Chinese prefer, they say, to purchase their food fresh each day. One of my professional friends, who could well afford to purchase a refrigerator or a television, chose not to do so because possession of such items would make him conspicuous in the apartment house and suspect perhaps of bourgeois tendencies. Furthermore, owning a private television set would remove him from group television watching in the lounge provided for that purpose on the ground floor of the apartment complex. And indeed, the prevalent attitude, a certain "keeping down with the Joneses," deviates noticeably from the usual practice in capitalistic countries.

Occasionally various branches of city families live in adjoining apartments in a housing complex. Factory workers may retire early with about one-half of their maximum salary. Such older, but still vigorous, retired people have enough money to maintain their apartments; they no longer work but can engage in civic and family activities. In one apartment we visited, grandparents share their two-room apartment next to that of their children with two of their grandchildren. The older couple likes to shop and cook and by taking care of such domestic chores enables the entire group to eat together every night in the grandparents' apartment—much to everyone's satisfaction.

Since almost all Chinese women work, whether a family prepares its meals in the apartment or eats in the nearby factory canteen depends largely on the possibility of such arrangements. Certainly eating at home is conducive to the maintenance of close family ties. Yet, even in the absence of home cooking and the socializing environment of the home dinner table, the family can eat together at the canteen and return to the apartment, where there are probably many evening hours available for family activities, which also consume a good share of workers' days off. In all museums, parks, and other public facilities that we visited, family groups dominated the scene. Hard-working Chinese mothers and fathers display great tenderness and solicitude toward their children; witness the scrubbed faces and bright, clean clothes—above all, the gentle attitude with which they are treated. Never did we see a child spanked or in tears; never did we hear a parent's voice raised. In fact everything we observed points to the continuance of the old Chinese traditions of family life among urban dwellers.

Eating all meals in the canteen at 12 to 15 yuan per person per month would cost a family with three children roughly one parent's total monthly wages. By Western standards, wage earners cannot afford to spend 50 percent of their total monthly income for food alone, but since rent, utilities, taxes, and insurance are minimal expenses, the Chinese can eat in the canteen with money to spare for other needs.

What is more, consumer goods to buy with that money are increasingly available. We were surprised to find whole streets in Peking, Shanghai, and Canton set aside for shopping. One such street was a five-minute walk from the Peking Hotel, and we frequently went there by ourselves to window-shop and to make purchases in a large department store.

The store is centrally located in the mall and surrounded on both sides of the always-busy street by many smaller specialty shops. An arcade, covered over by an arched roof of a sky-blue plastic material, cuts between the store and the building next to it. At the end of the arcade, well back from the street, is the store's main entrance. Its large single floor is divided into departments for clothing, yard goods, kitchenware, clocks and watches, cameras, sporting goods and games, books, stationery, tools, canned foods and candy.

Unquestionably, Chinese workers can easily procure all the essentials of life but as yet have little access to luxuries. Absent completely are the gadgets and trinkets that so attract American shoppers. In the kitchenware department we noticed especially the handsome big cast-iron kettles and enamelware pots and bowls in every color and size but could find no toasters, fancy cutlery, or electric mixers. We saw no crockery but stacks of porcelain in decorative patterns and quantities of blood-colored lacquer ware.

Clothing sections are departmentalized by type of wear, not wearer. Trousers, shirts, jackets, shoes, socks, hats, scarves, gloves, sweaters, and coats abounded all in basic plain styles. But obviously many Chinese women produce much of their family's clothing at home, for the yard-goods department, most attractive of all, with its huge bolts in all colors and patterns, seemed the busiest place in the store. The aisle in the shoe department was glutted with shoppers kicking off the old to try on the new.

When Dale requested some trousers, the obviously experienced gentleman clerk eyed her carefully and handed her a suggested size. In response to her questioning glance, he indicated there were no fitting rooms and, politely, that she could perhaps pull them on under her dress, but by this time we had attracted a sizeable number of onlookers, and it seemed wisest to buy them without a try-on.

The many clerks provide immediate, unfailingly kind and helpful service to Chinese buyers and foreigners alike. Their services are necessary, as all merchandise is stored in shelves behind the counters. They wrap all purchases meticulously in dun-colored paper and string, and buyers carry them off in string or straw bags.

Always crowded, the store maintained nonetheless an unhurried, pleasant atmosphere that pervaded the small stands that line the arcade as well. Here such services as shoe repair and a barber shop are provided, and various snacks are purveyed to passersby—soup, ice cream, soft drinks, tea, and noodles, the latter ladled out to customers who pick up their own bowls from the stack on the counter. Street cleaners hover in constant attention to sweep up

All manner of basic consumer goods abound at this Peking department-ment store. The lines are small, the service is courteous, and the shoppers buy eagerly.

This corner near a Peking shopping mall is always busy, as copies of Jenmin Jihbao, the People's Daily *newspaper are posted in the glass enclosed cases.*

rinds, papers, and all types of litter and to straighten up the benches and chairs.

Near the arcade groups of people are always congregated at a wall on which is posted a copy of Peking's daily, and only, newspaper, *Jenmin Jihbao*. Although copies of the newspapers are sold in newsstands, they are read by most city dwellers at such postings in prominent locations throughout all the cities. They are not sold to foreigners, who are forced to rely for news on a government-approved daily digest distributed through their hotels.

In the specialty shops near the large department store, we found a hat shop that provided us with the wide straw *tsao mao* we used at Lugou Ch'iao. Photo supplies, medical supplies, and antiques are sold separately. We were disappointed in the bookstore's lack of variety in its Chinese volumes, all bound monotonously alike; we lamented the rather banal photographs of Revolutionary dramas and, of course, the scarcity of foreign titles. Nowhere did we see records or record-players.

All the stores are government owned and operated with the result that they do not compete, offer little brand selection, and never advertise. Although the government depends on the markup for revenue, the prices are low, and the obvious intent is to provide a service to the people.

All work and no play? Almost, but not quite.

Theatrical entertainment, though limited to the nine Revolutionary dramas, can be seen regularly. We saw a film of the most widely known of all, "The Red Detachment of Women," at a Cantonese neighborhood theater, which was filled to capacity with an enthusiastic audience. The viewers were there to enjoy themselves. They came in groups, threes and fours, rarely a couple, and no one alone. Boisterous, youthful, they stood up to wave and yell at friends across the theater, stared at us with overt curiosity, but were all rapt attention when the movie began.

At the Peking Opera House we saw "Taking Tiger Mountain by Strategy," a stylish live performance by extremely competent singers and actors. In Shanghai's most elegant repertory theater we took in "The White-Haired Girl" (to my mind the best of the dramas), but the fervor of the audience did not vary when we watched the filmed version with our friends on the commune.

Most of these dramas were written soon after Liberation but

Workers and their families enjoy the parks scattered liberally in all of China's cities. Here at Hangchou they can view a huge ancient Buddha at a small museum.

have been updated in recent years to pound home more effectively the sentiments of the Cultural Revolution. All have been encouraged and approved by Ch'iang Ch'ing, Mao's wife and a former actress. The plots always concern the struggles of the courageous, the indomitable, the dedicated server of the people against the evil, the conniving, the decadent landlords and petty bourgeoisie. In "The White-Haired Girl," the young heroine escapes her evil landlord master by running away into the forest, where she lives in great hardship for many years until discovered and rescued by a patrol of the Red Army. Not one but nine ballerinas dance the role in this ballet, as The Girl ages (and her hair whitens), a conscious de-emphasis of the "star" tradition. All nine heroines take a bow at the end of the production. Even the very newest drama, "The Song of the Dragon River," does not deviate one iota in its story of heroic peasants in an agricultural brigade who form a human dam to divert a flood from land endangered by an earlier landlord's exploitation. Politics is in command. These stereotyped melodramas all too clearly reinforce the Maoist line, but that they afford a most welcome glimpse of beauty, music, talent, and showmanship cannot be denied. Their songs are the ones everyone knows and sings—their style and plots crop up in every home talent or school theatrical in the country.

Following the technical traditions of Oriental opera, long the most popular art form in China, the voices are shrill and hard, the faces freeze into the proper mask for expressing each emotion, and the bodies perform stylized movements with mechanical precision. Western reaction to these dramas is apt to be negative. The competence and discipline of the actors, singers, and dancers are nonetheless unquestionable; they have been well trained; what is more, they are attractive young people who perform with genuine verve. All mechanical aspects—staging, lighting, and shooting and editing of film—compare favorably with sophisticated work anywhere.

Little by little other cultural advantages have been made available to the citizenry at large. In 1971 we were guided privately and alone to see the Ming and Ch'ing dynasty treasures of the

This Canton family is enjoying one of the parks newly opened to the pleasure of the masses, along with a prized, and only recently obtainable, possession—a camera.

Volleyball in a Hangchou park. Emphasis on exercise and the prevalence of a balanced, simple diet has helped China become a nation of healthy people.

Forbidden City. By 1972 it had been opened to all as the Palace Museum, displaying proudly the precious objects produced by Chinese artisans, albeit with abundant and prominent reminders that all had been achieved at the cost of peasant starvation and abuse during the years of imperial rule. Bus tours travel frequently north from Peking to the Ming tombs, Great Wall, and other archeological sites. Such cultural breaks in the monotony of everyday life are few and far between. They represent a tie with elements in Chinese history that leaders of the New China can recognize only in the context of useful instruction about the evils of the past.

Physical culture, on the other hand, enjoys top ranking as both an organized and an individual recreation. Young and old alike radiate fitness and vigor. In Peking, while staying at the Hsin Ch'iao Hotel, I often walked the several blocks to a nearby park, sometimes in the very early morning hours. Always I found large numbers of citizens engaged in exercises. The older people, especially the men, generally were executing a series of graceful balletlike movements, called *tai-chi-chuan* (sometimes incorrectly referred to as "Chinese shadowboxing"), a routine carefully designed to exercise and coordinate every muscle of the body. On its completion, each movement is held in its graceful pose for ten to fifteen seconds before the next is begun. No one seemed the least self-conscious about performing such exercise in public, and watching them in the quiet of a Peking morning was like attending a gigantic pantomime.

Younger people engage in more vigorous exercises—running or calisthenics. Every morning before their studies or work begin, schoolchildren and factory workers congregate in open spaces throughout the cities for group exercises—deep knee bends, push-ups, bending and jumping—usually led by Red Guards. This type of exercise, plus walking and the constant use of bicycles, is building a healthy nation. Certainly there are few excessively fat people, although many Chinese have broad frames and husky builds. Frequent exercise and the prevailing simplicity of a diet low in fats and sweets and abundant in fresh vegetables provide a balanced physical life and minimize the problems of heart disease and obesity, which constitute such a menace to middle-aged and older people in more affluent Western societies.

In addition to participating in exercises and sports, the Chinese are eager spectators at competitions. We lived across the street from a basketball arena during one stay in Peking, and almost every night crowds of people assembled to watch games between teams from various schools and factories. At Peking's magnificent sports palace, a crowd of ten thousand is not unusual for gymnastic competitions.

While wandering in the streets of Peking, we occasionally noticed groups of children or factory workers with knapsacks on their backs, obviously headed for the open country. Sometimes they were on their way to what we would call a camping trip, during which younger children could learn how to exist without the normal accouterments of city life. At other times, such forays were directed to a special project for which the group had volunteered, like tree-planting or terrace-building in the countryside, earth-moving to construct levees or dams, or even road-building. Such expeditions undeniably bespeak a paramilitary intent and are probably considered an adjunct to developing vigorous soldiers and high morale.

In China, as in all nations, life styles in the city and the countryside differ perceptibly. We found the Chinese peasants franker, more open, easier to approach, and quicker to smile than their counterparts in the cities. Yet, like their country cousins, city dwellers live at one with their surroundings. The factories form a core around which neighborhood life and morale is centered. Everyone knows the teachers, the barefoot doctors, and the marshals within this enclave. They can conveniently avail themselves of such facilities as stores, hospitals, and canteens. Above all, they take intense personal pride in the role they themselves have played in their improved status. They emphasized to us repeatedly that, through the elected Revolutionary Committees, they can institute changes in factory routine, albeit with the approval of the Communist Party branches and higher Revolutionary Committees. Nominally, at least, they are not free to change residence or job, but in spite of that and of their restricted political and intellectual freedom, the Chinese masses seem to enjoy a greater measure of control over those agencies that directly affect their daily lives than do most Western city workers.

All China today credits Chairman Mao for the inspiration of the new educational system. These students might be attesting their concurrence as they pose beneath the huge Mao poster on the library at the Academia Sinica in Shanghai, each one holding a copy of the "little red book."

[162]

8

The Masses Go to School

CHINA CONTINUES to be a society in flux. According to many competent observers, and even Premier Chou En-lai, the Cultural Revolution, impetus for much of the present upheaval, is not yet concluded but merely at a plateau—a statement certainly borne out in the remarkable changes that occurred during the few months between my 1971 and 1972 visits.

The philosophy underlying such changes in modern China's educational system is epitomized in several directives, culled from the writings of Chairman Mao Tse-tung. Here they are in official English translation by Peking's Foreign Languages Press:

1. Education must serve proletarian politics and be combined with productive labor.
2. Our educational policy must enable everyone who receives an education to develop morally, intellectually, and physically and become a worker with socialist consciousness and culture.
3. While the main task of the students is to study . . . . they should not only learn book knowledge, they should learn industrial production, agricultural production, and military affairs. They should also criticize and repudiate the bourgeoisie.

4. It is still necessary to have universities. . . . However, it is essential to shorten the length of schooling, revolutionize education, put proletarian politics in command. . . . Students should be selected from among workers and peasants with practical experience, and they should return to production after a few years' study.
5. Besides meeting the needs of teaching and scientific research, all laboratories and affiliated workshops of engineering colleges which can undertake production tasks should do so to the best of their capability.
6. To accomplish the proletarian revolution in education. . . . The workers' propaganda teams [and PLA] should stay permanently in the schools and colleges, take part in all the tasks of struggle-criticism-transformation there, and lead these institutions. In the countryside, schools and colleges should be managed by the poor and lower-middle peasants, the most reliable ally of the working class.

What could be clearer? The educational system of China, available to all, irrespective of class or work background, and compulsory for all children until approximately age sixteen, is designed to produce "the new socialist man," educated in order to better serve his people and country. All knowledge is to be directed to serving the people's needs; in fact, the distinction between students and workers is to be abolished in the formal sense. "Putting politics in command" means that political considerations permeate the educational experience from earliest childhood to the last year in school and on throughout a lifetime and that the dispassionate assessment of conflicting theories will be abandoned —in short, a positive contradiction of the Western educational ideals of the training of thinkers and the pursuit of knowledge for its own sake.

This philosophy was not spawned without strife. By 1959 education in China had reached a peak of elitism modeled on Soviet practice. In an effort to keep pace technologically by training only the most brilliant students, admissions policies increasingly emphasized competitive entrance examinations. The result was that 70 percent of the students were drawn from bourgeois and landlord backgrounds, reinforcing education as a one-class institution.

These policies were supported by Liu Shao-ch'i, then head of state, as compatible with his ideas of putting "technique in command." Discontent with this elitism made a dynamic contribution to the surge of criticism that culminated in the Great Proletarian Cultural Revolution.

It is said to have begun in Shanghai on November 10, 1965, when a political cadre, Yao Wen-yuan, with the aid of Mao Tse-tung's wife, published an article, "On the new historical play, 'Hai Jui Dismissed from Office.'" The article questioned the play's attack on Mao and its defense of the right-opportunist line (a political path that for opportunistic reasons adopts organizational patterns and techniques from rightist—that is, capitalist—systems). Mao's forces were unable to get this article published in Peking because of the repressive tactics of Liu and his Peking Party Committee. But finally it was reprinted in Peking in the *Liberation Army Daily,* and Liu's party could no longer restrain the mounting criticism. The ideological debate was thus opened to the entire nation and led to the struggle in which Liu (China's Khrushchev) fell from power.

After this first incident, six young professors in the philosophy department at Peking University took up the cause. They daringly covered the outer wall of the dining hall with posters written in giant characters that demanded to know why public debate on the questions raised in the play had been suppressed in the Peking press and Peking University. "We absolutely won't allow you to do it," read the gigantic accusations, as the cadres and teachers went on to blame Lu P'ing, president of the university and a supporter of Liu, for their own particular grievances. Lu P'ing attempted to divert them to a more academic debate and, failing that, mobilized sympathetic worker and student forces to crush the dissidents. Armed conflict broke out on the campus, and the dissension spread to other schools and universities.

Groups of middle-school and university students sprang up, calling themselves Red Guards. With the encouragement of Mao, who accepted one of their red armbands, they traveled around the country to arouse the masses. They organized great debates. They adopted the *tatsubao* (giant-character posters) as their own special technique. Their aggressive actions and their inflammatory exhortations—"Struggle against those persons in authority who are tak-

[165]

ing the capitalist road," "Repudiate old ideas," "Transform education"—led frequently to bitter and bloody struggle. China was thus forced into a period of disruption—even chaos. Excess was committed on both sides, and much of it centered around educational institutions. After many months stability returned only when Mao sent groups of workers and soldiers into the universities. They effectively put an end to open combat between the two factions, not entirely by force of arms but by persuasiveness and conciliatory tactics as well.

Against this background of conciliation supported by force, the tripartite Revolutionary Committee was introduced. This shrewd innovation brought together university professors and students, political cadres from the ranks of the workers, and PLA personnel to work cooperatively to reorganize the universities.

From 1966 to 1970 the universities were closed as academic institutions, while the Revolutionary Committees met, discussed, and planned ceaselessly the formulation of a new educational policy that would implement the ideals of the Cultural Revolution and Chairman Mao's thoughts. By 1970 the framework had at long last been hammered out. Once again, students were admitted, but cautiously and gradually and not directly from secondary school but from factories, farms, and the army. Qualifications included not only unusual intellectual capacity but also the kind of political and social reliability emphasized by Mao and the Party. The projection is that by 1974 the universities will have reestablished full operating capacity but will offer a reduced time schedule and a curriculum diverted increasingly to practical knowledge and applied studies. In consequence, these same ideas have percolated down from the universities through all the years of the educational process.

Translated into current practice, the effect of Maoist theory and the Cultural Revolution is that from the moment of birth, the average Chinese child experiences socializing influences unknown to most Western children. The first stage is the crèche, or nursing room, a service to be found in all factories and most communes. Here working mothers deposit their babies each day and, from this time forward, these children are constantly members of a group. Their surroundings are sanitary and commodious—plain walls, curtainless windows, bare floors, and little furniture. Their

From the age of a few months all Chinese city youngsters (and many on communes too) spend every day at a nursery. Their care is wholesome, and they learn early on to be cooperative members of a group.

physical needs are attended to carefully by trained workers in identical white uniforms whose patience and affection is extended equally to all the children. They spend their days sleeping or simply vegetating in cribs lined up in rows across the room. When they are old enough to walk, they take their meals, go outside to play, and receive their toilet training at scheduled times all together. They are provided with few, if any, toys. In some nurseries, mothers visit their children for a short period each day.

In the nursery schools, which engage the lives of young Chinese from about two and a half to six years of age, training emphasis advances from the sense of group to mutual aid. At an age when many Western children are still at home, deprived of regular peer companionship, Chinese children are being guided into experiences that teach concern for their fellows. They learn to button not only

[167]

Children do everything together in the day care nurseries: above, toilet training, and below, nap time.

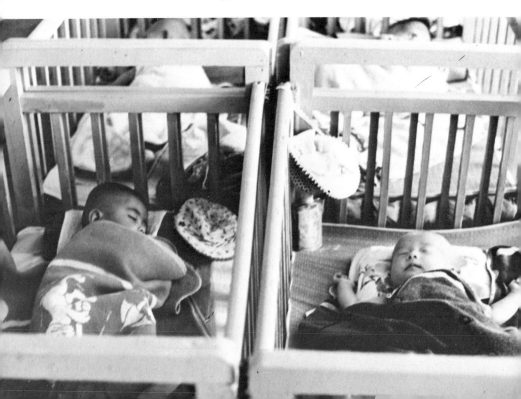

their own but other's clothing. Their toys tend toward functionality. Hence toddlers learn to plant seeds and pull weeds in shared garden plots. They take turns pulling each other in little wagons. In the sandpile they gravely pass the shovels back and forth; throwing sand is unheard of. When their groups take walks, each child holds another's hand, not entirely because such conduct facilitates control, but partly because they are being taught concern for the other's welfare.

The hours that each child spends at these schools are arranged according to each mother's work schedule. Children may come any time after 6:00 A.M. and go home any time between 4:00 and 9:00 P.M., a plan that takes into consideration not only the mother's working hours but also her desires about cooking family meals and her attendance at meetings after work. By the time they enter kindergarten and elementary schools, Chinese youngsters are used to associating with peer groups and spending most of the day away from parental influence.

The organization and procedures in the primary and lower-middle schools we observed on the Lugou Ch'iao commune are typical of the several city schools we saw. In all of these, disciplinary problems appear to be minimal or even nonexistent, which may be related to the children's early acceptance of the group as a natural medium for development. Through the group experience, the glorification of "our Helmsman, Chairman Mao," and the repression of individual aspirations for the good of the group easily become the inescapable focuses of educational life. Service to country requires that skills in mathematics, science, and the vocational arts and crafts be well taught, while critical studies of world history, other cultures, or conflicting interpretations of art and literature be minimized. The child emerging from this system is likely to be more conforming and less independent in his thinking than a Western child. He is likely to grow up with a strong sense of social responsibility and duty to his production unit and country as well as a strict and somewhat puritanical moral sense. Above all, his ambition for personal advancement will be replaced by a desire to see his group advance.

Both the curriculum and the students' behavior are strictly organized and completely controlled by central authorities. It reminds me of the regimented educational practice to which I was exposed as a child in the 1920s, which I remember still with

School is serious business. The chemistry class at a Lugou Ch'iao lower-middle school accords the teacher perfect attention.

distaste. Yet the Chinese students seem not to question it. They manifest only strong determination to become educated and trained and thereby to "serve the people." Education, traditionally denied their parents and grandparents, is finally miraculously available to them. There are no boundaries limiting that training, so long as the people do not question the system. And the system has provided such continuing improvement in the lives of the people that even the students, whose Western counterparts are the most visible questioners, have no desire to oppose it.

A description of one institution that my wife, daughter, and I visited will perhaps illuminate particularly well a comparison of the Chinese and American educational systems. The Ching An Children's Palace in Shanghai is one of several similar institutions organized to give extracurricular training to exceptionally meritorious students, who have been selected for the honor by their teachers and fellow students. We spent an afternoon there visiting classes for children of about nine to eleven years old, from the primary school system, although a few were slightly older—about thirteen—and might have been from lower-middle school.

Even lower-middle school has its practical side. These three young Red Guards (witness the armbands) are making acupuncture needles.

Quite appropriately, the Palace is situated on the grounds of a magnificent nineteenth-century estate, formerly the property of a Western capitalist and confiscated by the People's Republic for its present use. Our guides, enthusiastic, efficient students, met us with the inevitable handclapping at the gates and conducted us to the main building, the mansion itself, and, past nooks and crannies, into the countless classrooms supplied by its Victorian architecture. Two interpreters moved at our elbows throughout the tour, aspirating a running commentary in perfect English, supposedly a translation of the strident remarks of our guides.

Activity—intense, constant, tightly structured—is the watchword at the Children's Palace. The two thousand special students are trained intensively in carpentry, painting, model-building, weaving, singing, dancing, instrumental music, and recitation. Our guides determined that our pace should match that of the glutted schedule of their school and hurried us from class to class, allowing no opportunity for reflection or a second glance.

In the painting class, the boys were at one table, the girls at another; bent in concentration over their pictures, they were neatly filling in marked areas with preselected colors. There was no free drawing, finger painting, or clay modeling. In carpentry we watched these specially chosen youngsters assemble precut models, wielding hammers, saws, and glue with awesome dexterity. But no one was constructing a simple gift or a creative form of any kind. Their dancing instruction resembled precision drill. They made few mistakes, and there was no improvisation.

The crowded passageways, the rush, the high noise level created an atmosphere of constant din that climaxed in the orchestra rehearsal room. Again, drill it was, but in this case sheer volume overpowered cadence. Oddly, in the midst of a crashing rendition of a Revolutionary drama tune, we noticed at least one student whose enthusiasm had palled; a little fellow playing a kind of bass viol stared into space in utter boredom at another performance. Yet, on the whole, the children were zealous and cheerful; they seemed to thrive on close supervision and crowded schedules.

In one classroom we were astounded to find some of these nine- to eleven-year-olds practicing acupuncture on each other. They had obviously been drilled in the location of effective acupuncture points in the arms and legs. They confidently sterilized

Chingan Children's Palace provides after-school enrichment programs for specially selected Shanghai students. Some of the youngest greeted us at the gate.

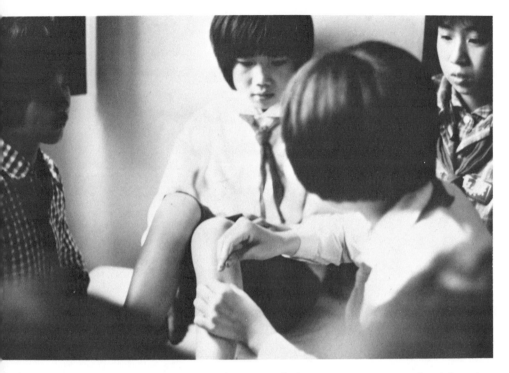

The curriculum at Chingan includes acupuncture practice (above) and (below), less unexpectedly, model building.

needles and inserted them in the proper points. The acting patients reacted with a slight twitch or a quick "o-o-oh" when the proper tingling sensation indicated that the needle had found its mark. None of them seemed fearful of the experience, and, indeed, all engaged in it willingly. Such practice would also seem to prepare the youngsters for stoic acceptance of pain in a future medical emergency.

Following our inspection of the various activities inside the main building, we were taken outside to observe groups of children working in garden plots and running an obstacle course. In the latter exercise, the children demonstrated great agility and fearlessness. They hurdled and dodged around obstacles; they balanced easily across tightropes and narrow planks; they slithered on their bellies under barbed wire. The course undoubtedly develops good coordination and strong bodies, but its implications for training in military discipline were all too obvious.

Returning to the building, we entered a large ballroom of yesteryear, in which folding chairs had been arranged to effect a small auditorium. Seated in the front row with our interpreters right behind us, we were treated to a demonstration of the performing arts. There were others in the audience, students and a few parents, but we were the honored guests. The announcer stared straight out over our heads and fairly bugled the introduction to each number. There were dances, tableaus, a short play, and songs by a chorus. The style in each was derived from the Revolutionary dramas. The dancing, professionally but mechanically executed, gave the children the aspect of puppets on strings. Their youthful voices, in singing and in speech, had been trained to achieve the constricted, hard tone typical of the Chinese opera—brilliant, but lacking in nuance. We applauded their agility and amazing perfection.

By far the greatest emotional impact of the visit came when we returned to the conference room for tea and refreshments. Seated at a long table facing about twenty persons, we were encouraged to ask questions of the group, which included not only the RC but also certain selected students—the cream of the cream, as it were. At each of our questions, hands flew up, youngsters jumped to their feet, all eagerly striving to supply the necessary information. Often, when more than one responded, it was neces-

A student performance at Chingan featured a dramatic ballet about the abacus.

sary to restrain the others so that one of them could in fact answer the question. I have never before seen such enthusiasm for a school exercise. Furthermore, their answers were delivered in such loud, stentorian tones that we wanted to cover our ears. Chinese classroom procedure everywhere demands that recitations be sung out loud and clear, and the practice reaches its peak at the Children's Palace.

The children told us that their days start at 6:00 A.M. Even before breakfast they are out in the lanes doing exercise drills organized for neighborhood groups by the Young Pioneers or Red Guards to the instructions of a radio broadcast. They spoke glowingly of the routine opening exercises of their regular schooldays —twenty minutes devoted to readings from Chairman Mao, after which the students recount their activities of the previous day. Each one strives to relate his experiences to the teachings of the

Chairman and to illustrate how he has bettered himself for service to the people.

On the three days a week they go to Ching An, the children have only four morning classes of forty minutes each—in arithmetic, history, language, and composition. On other days there are five lessons, three in the morning, two in the afternoon, ending at 2:20 in the afternoon, after which there is an hour for "mutual small groups"—special sessions during which slow learners are assisted in their schoolwork under the tutelage of their brighter peers. We were heartened indeed to learn of this remarkable and useful application of Mao's dictums on mutual aid—the first time we had heard of a concession to, or even acknowledgment of, the needs of atypical children.

Upon seeing our interest, the students themselves elaborated. No matter how a child is hampered in normal school progress—he may be a slow learner, he may be hyperactive or painfully withdrawn—he is turned over to his more typical classmates for help. Example and persuasion are the approved methods by which he is urged to adopt a behavioral mode that is considered more desirable for the group. The children, and their elders, insisted that such techniques inevitably succeed. It suggested Skinnerian reinforcement: "If you go along with the group," the lesson seems to say, "you will get along and be accepted by your fellows. If, however, you deviate, we will continue to work on you to get you to conform." Judging by the enthusiastic discipline of the models at the Children's Palace, the pressure to conform must be practically irresistible.

They recited other activities with pride. There are opportunities for special military training. Sometimes they report to factories for instruction and work. A young Red Guard volunteered that children in one primary school put together and manufacture such simple items as mosquito nets. The children at another school learned so much about herbal medicine that they were able to treat some of each others' minor illnesses.

The children emphasized that, although final examinations are given in school and grades are received, these are not the main criteria for advancement. Attitude toward the group and morals are more important. Many children, for example, show their cooperative nature by volunteering to help physically handicapped

[177]

A conference with students and RC members in a room presided over by pictures of Marx, Engels, Lenin, Stalin, and Mao concluded our visit to Chingan Children's Palace.

children. Some even constructed a special cart for a lame child and now vie for the responsibility of his daily care.

"But what," my wife asked, "is done for the deeply troubled child—what are the psychological resources for treatment of the truly aberrant?" The question seemed to fall on uncomprehending ears; no one knew how to grapple with it. The briskness faltered. There was another allusion to "mutual small groups." Someone else mentioned that a shy child would be helped by others living in his street or lane to accept responsibility to speak; all agreed that a child with emotional problems would be asked to repeat the sayings of Chairman Mao and, with sympathetic aid from his peers, would gradually gain confidence. No specially trained personnel are required for this therapy.

I asked whether the children giving these remarkably comprehensive answers were representative of their age group or had been chosen because they were especially bright or spoke exceptionally well. A thirteen-year-old replied that all children would react in much the same way, because their training enables them to be confident and secure and to speak in public.

When we departed from Ching An, groups of children lined up and applauded us much as they had when we arrived. We, of course, applauded back. They seemed unsurprised by any aspect of our behavior, in fact, showed no curiosity about us at all. As we got through the gates and were beginning to savor our release from the pounding insistence of the Palace ambience, we heard another burst of applause. They were greeting another group of visitors before we were out of earshot. The impression that these children are constantly on exhibition and, in some sense, showpieces was unavoidable.

The Children's Palaces most definitely perform a valuable service in enhancing the skill and talent of selected children, but at Ching An the sheer number of visitors must seriously interfere with genuine progress. Even more important, if a student should possess outstanding creative ability, how could it be nurtured in an environment where he has no free time at all and is always under strict supervision? My wife and daughter came away certain that later on in life such children could easily be made to follow in lockstep whatever orders any leader issued to them. I, on the contrary, am not sure this is a valid extrapolation from what we observed. An emphasis on cooperation and mutual concern pervades education in China and would tend to foster attitudes of resistance to antihumane acts. That influence is surely as strong as the compulsion to conform. I must admit, however, to some disquiet over the possible effects of such a tightly organized educational system on the student's later ability to act independently.

Several other incidents confirmed our impressions of the Chinese educational philosophy as one that shuns foreign influence and differs dramatically from Western practice in its attitude toward unusual children. Before we left the United States, my wife had decided that an appropriate gift from America would be a large collection of typical children's books. Hopefully these books would give the Chinese some notion of the thought patterns and training modes that influence America's young. If any of them seemed suitable for the Chinese experience, then we hoped that Chinese-language translations and an accompanying boost to international amity might result.

Upon our arrival in Shanghai, we had confided to our friend Loo Shih-wei that we had a gift of books and wondered about the best way to make the presentation, to whom and where. Loo transmitted our intention to the local authorities, who promised to consider the matter and to report back to us. During the discussion at the end of our visit to the Children's Palace, however, we spontaneously offered some of the books to the RC there. To our great surprise, the offer was met with an impassive reserve. Thank you, but a careful investigation of the situation by appropriate authorities would be required before any books could be accepted. This surprised us, confused us, and in the end, somewhat saddened us. We finally made a formal presentation of the books to our host in Peking, P'an Ch'un of the Academy of Sciences and requested that they be turned over to the proper recipients. P'an thanked us profusely and warmly, yet no one mentioned these books again until we ourselves brought the matter up in the Great Hall of the People during a meeting with P'an's superior, Kuo Mo-jo. He too expressed pleasure on receiving the books, but we concluded that they would probably be ignored. We left with a sense of failure, and we still wonder whether Chinese children would enjoy *Winnie the Pooh, The Little Engine That Could, Blueberries for Sal, Make Way for Ducklings,* and *Old*

MacDonald Had a Farm. When we got to the commune, we distributed directly to the children some small, cloth "How to Do It" books. They were immediately successful, for they spoke a universal language, to which neither ideology nor politics could take exception.

While we frequently heard that deviant children are simply surrounded by sympathetic classmates and helped to return to the mainstream, we observed at least one instance of rather unfeeling treatment of a child. This was the four-year-old son of number-two son in the family compound on the Lugou Ch'iao People's Commune. He stood out from the other children immediately; for example, he was always bare-bottomed rather than clad in trousers of any kind. We assumed that this was because he was not yet toilet trained. He was extremely mischievous and always grinning slyly. We called him "the imp." Whenever there was any trouble in the courtyard, it was taken for granted that the imp was at the bottom of it. Even his mother and father treated him as though they didn't really expect him ever to behave like other children.

This puzzled us, for we found him unusually bright and appealing. An older cousin let slip a possible explanation. The imp had been born with two thumbs on his right hand; one had been rather skillfully amputated, leaving what appeared, at first glance, to be a normal hand. Closer examination revealed, however, that the remaining thumb projected at an awkward angle, which made it inefficient in grasping. Certainly this abnormality would be with him for the rest of his life, but why did such a small disability lead his family to adopt such a contrary attitude toward him? Was it that he would be unable to do his share of work in the fields as a member of the commune? Certainly the thumb was not that serious. Another likely explanation is that peasant wisdom associated the polydactyly with incorrigible behavior.

Because of fondness for the imp, we singled him out for special attention and affection. He responded eagerly to a bit of good old-fashioned cuddling and quickly learned to be front and center whenever we started our word play or music with the children in the courtyard. My wife and I both fleetingly considered asking if we could take the imp back home with us; and in fact his mother once jokingly suggested it. We wonder how he will fare in the future. When he enters school, will his classmates surround him and ease him into ordinary conformity and group acceptance? Or will the story of his physical deformity mark him an aberrant person for the rest of his life?

In sharp contrast to the mechanized, impersonal training of students at the Children's Palace and the seemingly casual attitude toward the imp was the extremely humane treatment of the children at a school for deaf-mutes in Peking. This school was set up in 1958 with untrained personnel and limited programs. Of the 230 resident students, 95 percent came from worker families and would ordinarily have received no treatment for their deficiency, incurred in most cases as a result of a severe ear infection at age two or three.

In 1968, during the Cultural Revolution, several doctors decided that new techniques were needed to help these children become truly educable. It was known that some types of deafness, especially those resulting from early childhood illness, were reversible. Because these children had not been able to hear when they would normally have learned to speak, they were also mute. If partial hearing could be restored, the doctors reasoned, then speech could be taught. Speaking, in turn, would lead to a greater appreciation of the nature of the sounds involved, which would improve lip reading and the hearing process. But how to go about curing deafness? The answer was acupuncture.

As the story was told to us, paramedical personnel of the PLA, guided by Mao's teaching, began to study the problem. Through repeated and sometimes painful experimentation on their own bodies, they eventually discovered that simultaneous insertion of acupuncture needles just back of the ear and into the forearm improved hearing, at least temporarily, in some cases.

We saw this treatment being administered in the school classrooms. Stoically, the children lay their heads down on their desks for the insertion of the needles; they winced as the tingling sensation started in their ears, but after the needles had been manipulated and removed, they immediately sat up straight again and responded to the teacher's questions. We were informed that acupuncture stimulation given at intervals over several days resulted in marked improvement in hearing for many of the children. In the three years since acupuncture treatment was initiated, six children have improved sufficiently to be transferred to ordinary schools, and transfer is contemplated soon for eight others. Most students do not make such dramatic improvement but remain in the school and receive speech therapy as well as acupuncture treatment.

One young Red Guard, Yih Nai-shan, became a deaf-mute at the age of two after an infection and a high fever. Now nineteen, her hearing has been recovered somewhat after repeated acupuncture treatment. She spoke to us rather mechanically, in loud, understandable syllables. She first praised Chairman Mao; her life ambition, she said, is to go on to glorify Chairman Mao because he is responsible for her recovery. She and several other advanced students, who have shown spectacular improvement through acupuncture, presented recitations and even a short play.

On the walls in the classrooms were elegant large diagrams, demonstrating clearly the placement of the tongue, the teeth, and the lips for the pronunciation of the various sounds required for speech. Under each diagram were both the Chinese and the phonetic rendition of the sound. The teacher made frequent reference to these diagrams as she mouthed the syllables loudly and distinctly and had the class repeat after her. Some simple tricks were used to get important points across; for example, the sound *ch'i* was practiced by each child while holding a long strip of paper in front of his mouth. The sound was not considered correctly voiced unless the child's breath caused the paper to move.

The children evinced high spirits; many will surely make their way back into society. Their courage and determination is impressive. As they solemnly recited "Dare to think, dare to act" or "Fear nothing and be prepared to die," they appeared to be ready to undergo great personal hardships in order to conquer their abnormality.

The deaf-mute school we visited is but one of four such in Peking alone. Similar schools for children with sight difficulties as well as for those with hearing problems are found in every province in China. Student age ranges from eight to twenty. The schools are so well thought of that there are more applicants than places. Often children who cannot be admitted are given the same acupuncture therapy at home by barefoot doctors.

The uses of acupuncture as an anesthetic and analgesic agent

Students at the Deaf Mute School in Peking, having just received acupuncture treatment, are ready for speech lessons. Each has a "little red book." Learning is aided by the phonetic charts and mouth diagrams on the wall. The PLA members are acupuncture specialists.

are widespread and increasing in China. As to its actual success in the treatment for deaf-mutes, I cannot offer any proof but can only say that my hosts believe it works. On the other hand, I cannot concur with the view of some unsympathetic Westerners that the entire operation at this school is an elaborate charade, a show with no significance, for the spirit that prompts Chinese study and support for it is humane and sincere—and congruent with the current educational plan in China of providing schooling for all young people.

Completion of lower-middle school at age sixteen marks the end of formal education for most Chinese. By then they have received training in basic educational skills and a wide variety of socializing experiences through nursery school, kindergarten, elementary school, and lower-middle school. All but about 20 percent of them will start to work in factories or on communes. Further education will be limited to compulsory political indoctrination in their work units and some adult education at night school in the cities or during the slack periods of winter in the countryside.

The remaining 20 percent or more, who are selected for upper-middle school, receive an additional two years of study in mathematics, science, world history, and Marxism. Many students undoubtedly merit and desire university education at this point, but this is not available to them until they have proved themselves by serving the people. Such a policy might seem an interruption of the educational process but is completely acceptable to the young people in China. Imbued with Maoist philosophy, they eschew courses of action that might single them out as seekers of individual glory. At age eighteen, therefore, graduates of upper-middle school are required to spend at least three years with the masses learning the practical arts of food production, manufacture of consumer goods, or to do service in the diversified activities of the PLA. To be considered for admission to the universities, they must convince society during this period that they are good people, good workers, and good socialists, for it is upon the recommendation of their fellow workers that they are chosen.

Even after the two to four years given over to university training, most students return to field or factory to employ their knowledge in service. Some are appointed by the state to teach. A handful may continue as scholars in the Western sense, and these few all appear to be at the national research institutes in science or technology. I was able to garner little information about the place or the rationale for the scholar in the arts or in literature within the Chinese educational system. How can young adults, after exposure to the highest education that China can offer, return to life as workers? How can they be satisfied in such occupations when at least some of them must be drawn to pure research? Seeking answers to these questions was a main objective as I toured university campuses in China.

Although I had occasion to visit others, Peking University is the one I know best. The rapid changes at this institution between 1971 and 1972 testify to the transience of any fixed description of Chinese educational modes and typify very well the nature of university life today.

The campus is situated in the northwest suburbs in a heavily wooded park—a gracious background for its traditional architecture. The simple low buildings of buff-colored brick with their red-tiled roofs and curved and decorated drainage spouts nestle harmoniously in the rich, green pines. Entrance is through a quaint stone gateway onto an arched bridge over the stream leading to the quiet lake in the center of the campus, then down a long drive to the central buildings. Here a gigantic alabaster representation

A giant alabaster statue of Chairman Mao stands in front of the central campus buildings at Peking University.

of Chairman Mao stands omnisciently—a silent reminder that our surroundings are not solely for esthetic pleasure.

During both my visits, my host was Chou Pei-yuan, a mathematical physicist, who has worked at Caltech and MIT in the United States and speaks English fluently. Chou is vice-chairman of the Revolutionary Committee of the university and also a vice-president of the State Committee on Science and Technology, the host organization for most foreign scientific visitors. He is reserved and extremely intelligent—a Chinese scholar of the old school, who is now engrossed in the effort to deliver the traditional educational background by methods that conform to Maoist philosophy. He and I spent many hours strolling on the campus, and seeing the university under his aegis proved as enjoyable as it was enlightening.

Peking University, often called *Peita* (large northern one), is today a comprehensive arts and science training center, with emphasis on the arts, as ten of its seventeen departments are in the arts and only seven in science. The various departments comprise forty-two specialties. (At Canton's smaller Chungsan University, there are only nine departments.) The staff at Peking numbers more than twenty-one hundred (compared to Chungsan's nine hundred), two hundred professors and seven hundred junior teachers in residence, the remainder being occupied in research or training in the field. Maoist educational philosophy disapproves of separation of educators from the masses. In order to help workers with their problems, educators must know the work experience. Accordingly, the faculty rotates regularly from research to teaching to practical work, which means that at any given time, a good part of the staff is absent from the campus. Off-campus job assignments are made by having professors submit applications for the work they desire. A jury of colleagues then votes on the request and makes the decision.

The university was founded as an imperial college in 1898. In 1911 it moved to its present site, formerly that of Yenching University, and "continued to serve only the ruling classes" until Liberation in 1949. Shortly after that, Mao visited the campus. Chou showed me the markers inscribed with typical quotations that had been put up to commemorate that event. "Get united and struggle for building up the New China" and "Combine education with production"—exhortations that still today serve as guidelines to policy.

The tremendous struggles of the Cultural Revolution are never far out of mind on the campus at Peking University. We talked with two Red Guards: an attractive young woman, Pei Shiao-jui, and Ke Lei, a young man. They had been on opposite sides in the days of the struggle between the forces of Liu Shao-ch'i and Mao for support among the students, but their differences were reconciled when a Mao Tse-tung propaganda team of Peking workers was sent to the campus in 1968. Now they say they work and study together in harmony.

In September 1970, when the new policy for universities had been worked out, Peking University was the first to open its doors. More than 2,500 new students from the working class, peasantry, and the army were admitted. (Chungsan University in Canton followed closely behind, opening in December 1970 to 540 students. Its pre-Cultural Revolution student body also was smaller, 4,500 to Peking's 10,000.) In both universities students had qualified by their excellence in political ideology and application of Mao's thought to their lives. They had forged close links with the masses and demonstrated their willingness to serve the people. In addition, they were in good health, were at least twenty years of age, and had completed upper-middle school and three or more years of practical experience.

All students receive a stipend from the government. Although low, at 19½ yuan per month (the average worker's salary is about three times that amount), it permits students to live, though in a Spartan manner, without family aid. This universal program of direct government scholarships opens up the possibility of higher education to every young person. Conceivably some prospective students coming from poor families might feel the need to forego schooling in order to continue contributing their salaries to their families, but in view of the economic well-being of the great bulk of the population, such a situation would rarely arise.

Students and faculty alike claimed that some of the biggest changes upon reopening appeared in the departments of liberal arts. While these students had formerly worked for fame and personal distinction, they now aim to develop the physical, moral, and intellectual powers that will best serve the people.

[188]

Understandably, the curriculum includes large doses of Mao's philosophical works, the study of Marxism-Leninism under the rubric of social science, the history of the international socialist movement, writing practice, and physical exercise. Students denigrated the old teaching methods—too much spoon-feeding, rote recitation, and competitive testing. Now, they explained, a democratic "mass line" (an officially approved policy validated by wide popular support) functions in which both teachers and students learn and teach. Professors also learn from the suggestions and criticism of workers during their off-campus assignments.

Such ideologically oriented objectives contrasted greatly with the practicality of the applied science work I had observed at Chungsan University in Canton. There, for example, the Department of Biology operates a factory on campus, which students and professors helped to construct. In this ramshackle building, molds are grown on agricultural wastes from nearby communes and used in turn to produce antibiotics. We saw tetracycline drugs that had been produced by fermentation and were being extracted, purified, tested, and sealed in glass ampoules for sale to the Chinese government for domestic use. In the course of these operations, students receive some instruction in biology, chemistry, engineering, and economics and, on emerging from such a program, can put their training immediately to work—at least in the specific procedures they have learned. Though a Westerner might question their capacity for solving problems not so closely related to their fields or for asking the questions that would lead to more creative work, they have a concrete contribution to make to society.

Walking past a *Peita* dormitory in 1971, we attracted the attention of a number of students, who poked their heads out of the windows to stare at us. On the spur of the moment, I asked if we might enter and converse with them. Chou agreed, and we met about forty of the ninety-two political-science students resident in the dormitory, who crowded into a small room, furnished only with two double-decker bunks along parallel walls, two desks, and two chairs. They offered us hot water to drink (tea being a luxury not possible on student stipends) and freely answered all our questions.

The male students live on the ground floor of such dormitories, teachers on the second floor, and females on the third floor—a true

Learning through doing at Chungsan University. Tetracycline is actually manufactured for sale. The picture above shows the ramshackle factory building put up at the program's inception by the students and professors themselves, and the one below, the new building, recently built from profits on the sale of their product.

cordon sanitaire if I ever heard of one. The class schedule of six days a week is rigorous. Everyone rises at 6:00 A.M. and participates in physical exercises, both organized and free, for half an hour. Breakfast at 7:00 is followed by classes from 7:30 to 10:00 and 10:15 to 11:30. Lunch and rest period last until 2:30 P.M., at which time classes are resumed until 5:30. Recreation, dinner, and free time follow until 8:00. From 8:00 to 9:30 there is a period of individual self-study, at 9:30 a group workshop, and by 10:00 it is bedtime again.

These mature students of the college of arts at China's leading university had come from various sections of the country, from agriculture, from industry, and from different classes in society. They spoke of their future lives in terms of Mao's dictum, "All our literature and art are for the masses of people." They expressed willingness, even desire, to return to their former jobs. There they would employ their training and talents to interpret the Revolution —to raise the cultural and political levels—for the people in their home communities. Were all these students in political science and language studies to become cadres? The limited need for teachers, interpreters, and radio and newspaper personnel will not employ many of them, especially since few such jobs require university training.

They did not even consider competing for those jobs that would seem more appropriate for persons so educated. In fact, when asked about competition between students, about grades and examinations and failure in courses, their response was laughter. No, no, they explained, examinations are only for the purpose of letting us know what we must learn better and showing the teacher what he has not taught so well. No grades are awarded, and there are no failures ever. All students cooperate to make sure that "not a single classmate is left behind."

By the time I returned in 1972, this policy had obviously been altered, after much criticism from teachers, who urged recognition of certain minimum academic standards. Not only had a grading system been reinstituted (with four grades: superior, fair, pass, and fail), but competitive examinations are being employed for both college entrance and jobs. The awarding of degrees, however, has not been reinstated at any level of educational achievement. Chou Pei-yuan stated that the needs of the state and those of the students are merged, so far as possible, in the assignment of positions. All jobs are judged equally valuable, and the university experience itself is considered simply an assignment that students receive on behalf of the state.

The campus itself had changed in 1972. The year before, dilapidated classrooms and laboratories testified to the disruptions of 1966–70. But now fresh paint, repaired windows, and mended furniture have restored more typically Chinese tidiness. New construction abounds as well. The new buildings have sacrificed some Oriental detail to the demands of functionality, but they still maintain the harmony of the architectural style. The busiest construction site is that of a massive underground shelter near the campus lake.

There are more students, though new 1971 admissions were cut back to only three hundred from the several thousand planned originally. The RC found they had not provided sufficient outlets for the practical work of so many students, and they decreased admissions to allow time for the expansion of connections with factories and communes and the development of more campus activities oriented to the problems of the masses. The number of new students in 1972, however, had been once again increased.

The objective is to build enrollment back up to its former eight thousand full-time and two thousand part-time students. About the size of my home university, Yale, I reflected, but that is almost the only similarity. The physical setting of *Peita,* not just the presence of trees and lakes, but the absence of automobiles, their clangor, and heavily trafficked streets, contrasts sharply, as does the social setting. Students are businesslike and purposeful—so serious, in fact, as to make the Yalie seem frivolous by comparison. They are also older by three to five years than typical American undergraduates. Carefree activities—dating, enjoyment of the weather or the out-of-doors for its own sake—do not infringe on the scheduled life at Peita.

By 1972 some subtle changes in these policies had also taken place. Chou's outward reserve slipped when he told me with obvious delight that thirty-eight students had been enrolled in a new curriculum, mainly in theoretical physics, a course which seems to parallel the study of basic principles found in physics departments anywhere. A new geology-geography-geomechanics

Peking University students practice microscope technique in a biology class.

program has also been set up with a similarly basic orientation. The teaching of biology, which had been devoted only to new applications for medical and agricultural techniques, is being expanded to include more traditional botany, zoology, and physiology. The operation of factories to delimit laboratory science at the university also seems to be on the wane, and there is now a shift to conventional academic subjects. For example, petroleum chemistry has been dropped from the curriculum, and in its place is catalysis, a subject that goes far beyond the process of cracking petroleum to include study of the universal chemical principles that underlie it. Chou Pei-yuan pointed out that this renewed emphasis on basic science was instigated by pressure from students and workers, not dictated by upper echelons. Unlike the situation in the primary and middle schools, curriculum choice is not dictated by national policy; one university may decide to offer theoretical physics, for example, while others may not.

[193]

I asked Chou for his appraisal of the overall effects of the Great Proletarian Cultural Revolution. He said that he had no doubt that in the short run the cessation of training during those years would cause deficiencies in the science program. In the long run, however, science would emerge with better direction and more vigor because of the avoidance of both revisionism and formation of intellectual elites removed from the masses. Chou, like most Chinese academic administrators, condemns the Soviet system of elitism and the training of an expert managerial class. The Chinese

Factory workers might seem out of place in university laboratories. Such is not the case with this pharmaceutical worker, temporarily studying basic chemistry at Peking University. He will return to his factory to use his new knowledge for its improvement.

admit the value of continuing education for workers but not of education to the extent that the goals of the educated deviate from those of the great mass of the people. They feel that a tripartite program of research, teaching, and practical work guarantees this unity. Furthermore, the opportunity to criticize professors at the periodic meetings of the Revolutionary Committee prevents the systematization of undemocratic educational practices.

Despite the recent trend to basic science, Chou had nothing but praise for the "July Twenty-first" universities, so named following a speech by Chairman Mao on that date in 1968, in which he cited an educational innovation of the Shanghai Lathe Factory. This factory originated a program that trains selected young workers for three years in new techniques as well as the broad, theoretical aspects of their work. These on-the-job seminars are taught by experienced workers and various university personnel. Successful thus far, the plan has spread to other factories. Chou explained that such continuing education is in line with the changes at the universities and will surely be employed advantageously on their jobs by skilled workers.

I asked what happens to a student who wants to go to a university and cannot get in. In answer, Chou Pei-yuan mentioned his own daughter who had attended an upper-middle school and works now in a beer factory. She had hoped to go on to a university, but her unit had never received an allocated university vacancy for which to recommend one of its workers. Chou contents himself that she can still improve her capacity to serve in other ways; she can become a cadre, for example, or take advantage of advanced training in the factory. But how does his daughter feel about this? Chou simply shrugged and smiled.

Conversations with several professional people revealed that their sons or daughters rarely followed in the parents' footsteps; most became farmers, laborers, or volunteers in advanced project work in the People's Liberation Army. Repeatedly I asked my hosts if this were a studied governmental policy to preclude an unbroken line of educational opportunities within any one family. Most denied that there could be such a policy, but the consistency of the pattern leads me to think otherwise.

Administration at Peking University is handled by a typical tripartite Revolutionary Committee of university personnel, cadres,

[195]

and PLA members, thirty-nine in all, who are entrusted with responsibility for the study of Mao's thought and the analysis of methodology to implement the aims of the Cultural Revolution. Candidates for the RC are proposed by the masses, that is, the faculty and students. I was assured that the candidates are discussed openly and that the elections are democratic. There are also RCs in each department in the university with duties similar to those of the chairman and executive committee in a Western university.

Chou was administrative head of Peking University when the Cultural Revolution sundered the campus between the forces of Mao and Liu. He admitted the instability of his own position at that time. Confronted by the two opposing factions, he had merely supported those groups with whom he was in agreement and had not attempted to influence others to his persuasion; this deprived him of the broad support he might otherwise have merited. He recognized this, and as a result of his own reeducation, he once again enjoys the unified support of the entire university community. He believes wholeheartedly in the tripartite Revolutionary Committee as the best administrative body for Peking University, while he admits that it has made some mistakes. For example, the faculty was underrepresented at first, and too much time was devoted to practical work on campus. These matters have been corrected, as others will be in the future, under a system so responsive to criticism. Like all the Chinese intellectuals I talked with, Chou reflected a thoughtful acceptance of the duration of time that might be required to effect all the educational changes suitable to the needs of the New China.

We also discussed the role of the Communist Party. Chou revealed that the Party branch on the campus prior to the Cultural Revolution had been dissolved and not replaced as such. Instead, small units have been organized within each department. According to the constitution of the Communist Party, membership in the Party is open to any eighteen-year-old Chinese worker, peasant, or any revolutionary who accepts the constitution, joins a Party organization and works actively in it, carries out Party decisions, observes Party discipline, and pays membership dues. Applicants must be recommended individually by two existing members, fill out an application form, and be examined by a Party branch, which then seeks opinions of the masses inside and outside the Party. Approval of applicants is by the general membership of the branch involved and the next higher Party committee. The persons chosen are zealots, those proved the most active revolutionaries of all. They continually study Marxism-Leninism-Mao Tse-tung thought; they apply it in a living way by their own discipline, their skill at convincing and uniting others in the national interest, and their fearless criticism and self-criticism.

Chou then told me that Communist Party membership on campus at present totals thirty-eight hundred, or about 50 percent of all personnel. This percentage—so much higher than that found in any other segment of society—makes it seem as though the university is still regarded the prime source of leadership.

Not far from Peking University and on the same pleasant roadway to the northwestern suburbs is located China's leading technical and engineering university, Tsinghua. Although it was founded in 1911, its campus is quite new. Students and faculty together designed its unpretentious, utilitarian buildings in 1959, and they were completed just before the Cultural Revolution in 1966. Though the highrise architecture contrasts strikingly with

At Tsinghua University student dormitories are new, simple, adequate.

the buildings at Peking University, it certainly does not resemble the bold innovation seen on many American campuses.

My companions in touring Tsinghua were Chang-wei, vice-chairman of the Revolutionary Committee and a professor of mechanics, who spoke English very well; Ma Wen-chung from the Department of Thermal Physics; and a female professor of architecture, Kuo Tai-hung. They related with pride the accomplishments of their institution since the transformations of the Cultural Revolution. Many of these, they said, resulted from the farsighted wisdom of the RC, which had continually dared to introduce experimental reforms.

The university now has eleven departments: electronics, electric power, automation, precision instruments, machine building, radio engineering, engineering physics, engineering mechanics, civil engineering, chemical engineering, and hydraulic engineering. These departments offer forty-eight different specialties. The teaching staff numbered 400 before Liberation in 1949; at present there are 2,600 and over 5,000 office and staff workers. Before Liberation the student body was 2,000 at the highest; by contrast there were 12,000 students in the four-year curriculum before the Cultural Revolution; now students in the first and second years of a three-year program number 4,500. The total area of the campus is 500 acres; before Liberation the buildings provided one million square feet of floor space and since have expanded to four and one-half times that size. In addition to the main campus that I visited, Tsinghua has several provincial branches. There are also smaller polytechnical institutions in Sian, Tientsin, Nanking, Shanghai, Harbin, and Canton. That the government places high priority on science and technology is indicated by the existence of a central state plan for engineering that determines the number of schools and alters the policies as the needs of the state change. New technologies may be added to the curriculum on the recommendation of industry groups and university officials as well.

My hosts emphasized that the reeducation of faculty intellectuals through labor in factory and field was a necessary preparation for reshaping their specialties according to the dictates of educational reform. As a reciprocal act, workers have been invited to the university to supplement their practical knowledge with theoretical studies. Under the present system, each professor must alter-

[198]

nately teach, research, and engage in production on a flexible schedule tailored to his or her own needs.

Tsinghua operates factories on campus and also maintains close contact with forty different factories in various cities as a means of providing them with technical assistance. Students are frequently given leave of absence for this purpose. Thus, learning from books is combined with learning from direct experience as a basis for the analysis and solution of practical problems.

At Tsinghua students and faculty alike believe they have a democratic method of teaching, because entering students, armed with their three years of practical experience, feel free to challenge their teachers, thus creating an educational dialogue. Current procedures emphasize independent study, encouraged by frequent handouts of factual material by the teachers, which are followed up by open discussions. Examinations are predistributed open-book tests, in which disagreement and discussion of possible answers are encouraged—a system that permits the bright students to help those who are having difficulty. Completion of a course thus involves more than a regurgitation of the teacher's lectures; it stresses training in analysis.

Admissions procedures changed drastically between 1971 and 1972. Prospective students now initiate their own applications and indicate their interest in engineering; then they must be recommended by their work units and approved by their Revolutionary Committees. (Superior students are occasionally recommended for university education without initiating the request themselves, but this is rare.) Final approval by the RC of the university depends on an interview, which is really an oral examination probing the applicant's basic scientific and analytic abilities. Despite official disclaimers, it must be considered competitive, since Tsinghua admits only one out of every four applicants who have won the recommendation of their work unit's RC. Although this method is ever subject to change, and the standards and details may differ somewhat from place to place, it is the currently prevailing admissions policy.

Many small factories are in operation on the Tsinghua campus. In most cases faculty, students, and workers have combined their efforts to build (sometimes to design) the necessary machinery. Our hosts pointed out that this practice not only supplies the

[199]

Students learn lathe operation and other machine shop techniques in regular courses at Tsinghua University.

needed machinery (which might be difficult to acquire from other countries) but also educates the students in the process and creates a self-contained, independent operation. In one such factory, a transistor workshop, integrated circuits are produced—enough to supply the entire university's demand. Silica crystals are sliced, oxidized, engraved by diffusion, aluminum-coated, pressure-welded by ultrasonics, then tested and packaged. The entire process compared well with methods in general use everywhere. Twenty-eight transistors constitute each plate, and each unit has twelve plates; a general-purpose computer might require several hundred such plates. I also witnessed, in an unplanned demonstration, printed circuitry being welded into place under the control of a micromanipulator. In another workshop, some students demon-

[200]

strated pressure-welding and a computer-controlled lathe by inscribing "Long live the unity of the people of the world" on a blank piece of metal.

Clearly at Tsinghua the skills of the engineer have been harnessed to better serve the needs of the people. The department of acoustical physics, for example, contains an all-tile acoustic laboratory. Wall and ceiling panels for this parabolic-shaped room have been so designed that 80 percent of the sound is absorbed. Reverberation time is simultaneously decreased from 9 to 1.8 seconds, thereby greatly sharpening audibility. This paneling is now widely used in theaters throughout China. An illumination laboratory in this same department features a device that creates an artificial sky, under which models of industrial plants and public buildings are placed in order to test illumination schemes. This is accomplished by precisely located photo cells that measure light attrition.

The library at Tsinghua is supervised by a Professor Shih, who studied at Harvard from 1945 to 1948. It contains 1.3 million volumes, mostly general reference works accumulated before 1952, when Tsinghua began specializing in science. Although seemingly an excellent collection, many of the books probably could be put to better use if transferred to nearby Peking University. Nevertheless, the main reading room was crowded; it seats four hundred, and almost every chair was filled. In addition, each department maintains its own subject library.

In a political-science reading room, we found practically no contemporary foreign literature (although I did see such books as Edgar Snow's *Red Star Over China* and Anna Louise Strong's *The Chinese Conquer China* and, of all things, a biography of George Washington) but plenty of Mao—in seventeen foreign languages as well as Chinese. Beautiful books on ancient pottery were being exhibited at the library, and we saw a display chronicling the history of printing in China there as well. Included were the earliest known examples of Chinese characters, said to be thirty-five hundred years old, printed on bone and turtle shell; specimens of characters printed on bamboo from Han dynasty tombs, about two thousand years old; and examples of the first moveable type from the late eleventh century.

Following the tour, we adjourned for tea and more discussion.

I started by an attempt to sound out my hosts on the diminishing popularity of engineering and technology in the United States and described the disillusionment among certain scientists, especially the young, who feel that science is not harnessed to the major needs of society but is servant instead to the military and inconsequential gadgetry. My Chinese colleagues were incredulous that this could be true and could not discuss the problem. Similarly, on the subject of the threat of pollution, the Chinese scientists were doctrinaire and professed only a stolid faith in the ability of the socialist state to overcome whatever problems might arise. They stated blandly, "If you want to avoid air pollution, just distribute cities more." They do not ponder solutions to such problems because the problems are not yet acute in China—an indication of how effectively and dynamically Tsinghua exemplifies China's pragmatic approach to science.

Overall, this university and all the others in the Chinese educational system are providing a democratized and practical means of offering advanced training to a cross section of the young working people. They symbolize the egalitarian ideal that attracts and holds the loyalty of Chinese youth.

The nature of graduate study, however, is still undefined in People's China. Since the Cultural Revolution, policy makers have been unable to reinstitute the graduate schools in conformity with Mao's philosophy of education. Following such directives as the "mass line," the dissolution of the master-pupil relationship, and deemphasis of individual achievement is difficult at the level of graduate study, which, traditionally at least, requires original, individual research.

Even so, high-level scientific research persists in China. It is under the aegis of a science and education group, which is represented on the State Council, the supreme planning body of the central government, presided over by Premier Chou En-lai. The group is headed by Kuo Mo-jo, who sits on the State Council, thereby insuring science a singularly high status in China. Kuo is also the president of the Academia Sinica, the agency through which most research is actually carried on.

Unlike national academies of science in the United States and other Western countries, the Academia Sinica is not an elected, self-perpetuating, honorific group. It is rather a collection of so-

Research laboratories at the Botanical Institute of the Academy of Sciences in Peking apply sophisticated techniques to nationwide production problems. Dr. Liu, at left above, heads a laboratory investigating fruit storage. Below, the electron spin resonance apparatus for the Institute's photosynthesis research was made in China.

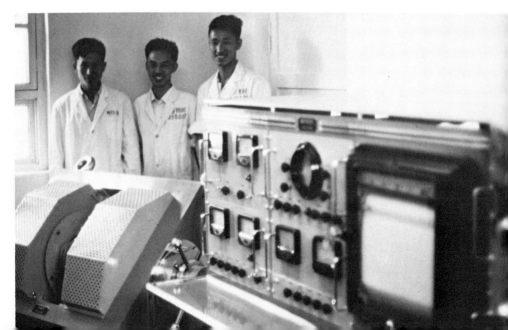

phisticated research institutes located throughout the country, to which distinguished scientists receive permanent appointments to carry forward the main thrust of investigations in their own fields.

In the course of my two stays in China, I observed the work at the Academy's Institutes of Botany, Microbiology, Plant Physiology, and Biochemistry. In 1971 scientific programs still suffered the severe dislocations caused by the Cultural Revolution. By 1972 a few excellent basic programs had started up again and are expected to regain their former momentum. The directors of these programs are all older men, trained and producing creditable research long before the Cultural Revolution, and scientists anywhere would take an interest in their work. Their libraries contain all the reference sources necessary for their current programs, although delivery of many foreign journals seemed to be running several weeks to several months late. Their laboratories contain much sophisticated equipment of foreign manufacture, as well as spectrophotometers, ultra-centrifuges, and electronic-spin resonance machines manufactured in China, although obviously copied from foreign models. Technicians abound in the laboratories, and the morale of the groups is high. Publication of scientific journals in China was suspended during the Cultural Revolution. It is being resumed only slowly, not because Chinese scientists are reluctant to share their work but because they fear the tendency of publishing to serve as a means of emphasizing individual achievements.

Several old friends, whom I had known in the United States as graduate students or postdoctoral fellows, and who speak English very well, briefed me on the operation of a typical research institute. Regular meetings of scientists with members of the Revolutionary Committees are held every few weeks to assess progress and to decide on new paths for the future. Drastically new pioneer research programs can be suggested at intervals and may be implemented if the group decides that the approach conforms to their basic mission and has some promise of success. All projects are evaluated and their future direction decided at the end of each year in democratic discussion. This struck me as a reasonable and effective procedure—one that might well be followed in the United States by either government or industrial research laboratories.

In the absence of university graduate education, these insti-

The organic synthesis laboratory at the Institute of Botany in Peking has the potential for high quality work.

tutes now suffice as the main training grounds for scientific leadership. This seems to consist of a rather loosely defined system of apprenticeships, filled from the ranks of workers and students. Older Chinese scientists realize the need for a clear-cut program for discovering and selecting brilliant young scholars if China is to produce scientists and engineers of the number or the caliber required in a society moving toward a more complex technology. They assured me they are slowly resolving the problems and developing such a system.

That science contributes successfully to daily life in China and that those persons with a scientific education enjoy a securely integrated role in the national scheme is obvious. How historians, poets, and artists contribute and what rationale exists for education in the arts and letters remain unanswered questions. I asked one of my interpreters for the names of some important new Chinese writers. She named no names, merely stating that "new young writers are emerging from the factories and the communes." The name of the book in China is "The Thoughts of Chairman Mao"—the purpose of literary education, to teach everyone to understand it. When I asked the same highly educated woman what American writers she knew, she mentioned Henry Wadsworth Longfellow, Mark Twain, and Jack London. The latter two were well known to several other interpreters as well. Not one recognized names like Ernest Hemingway, Eugene O'Neill, or William Faulkner. It seems that not only is literary creativity stifled but cultural insularity is imposed—as we observed so often in browsing in bookstores. Even educated Chinese seem only vaguely interested in learning more about America unless such knowledge promises direct application to Chinese affairs.

In spite of certain deficiencies, however, the facts are quite clear: the People's Republic of China has a definite educational objective—the training of socialist man and woman—and has fashioned an effective mechanism to implement it. The masses support the system enthusiastically. They've tried it and they like it.

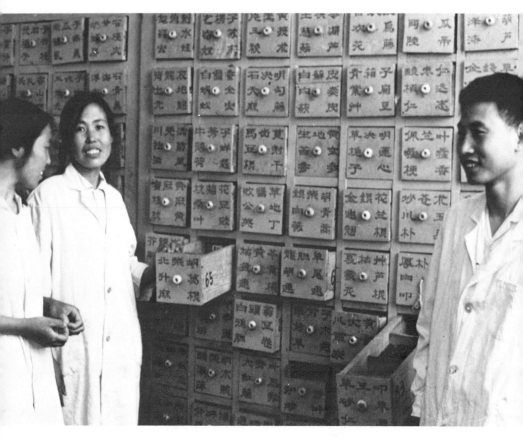

Herbal medicine has advanced far beyond the lore of old wives' tales in China. At Lugou Ch'iao's new hospital, the herbal pharmacy was well stocked and organized.

9

Needles, Herbs, and Health for All

DR. JOSHUA HORN, a British surgeon who practiced in China between 1954 and 1969, wrote of his visit in the 1930s:

> Although it is more than thirty years since I first went ashore in Shanghai, . . . some impressions of the week I spent there are indelibly etched in my mind. . . . The swarms of beggars of all ages, whole and diseased, vociferous and silent, hopeful and hopeless, blind and seeing. . . . The prostitutes. . . . The poverty. . . . The rummaging in garbage bins for possible scraps of food. Scurvy headed children. Lice ridden children. Children with inflamed red eyes—with bleeding gums—with distended stomachs and spindly arms and legs. . . . The bodies floating down the river. . . .

But in describing conditions in 1969, Dr. Horn wrote:

> Active venereal disease has been completely eradicated in most areas and completely controlled throughout China.

How could this be possible in the country where disease ran rampant just one short generation ago? When I met Dr. Horn in New York in 1971, I questioned him closely about the accuracy of this sweeping generalization. He reiterated his statement and went on to say that in Peking it is now impossible to find active syphilitic lesions to demonstrate to medical students so that a generation of doctors is growing up in China with no direct experience of syphilis. Dr. Horn's claims have been corroborated by Dr. Victor Sidel, professor of community medicine at Albert Einstein Medical School, who visited China in 1971 and 1972. He has reported that the vital statistics for Shanghai indicate the complete absence of venereal disease in the city. These data, together with public health statistics on other infections and epidemic diseases, establish Shanghai as one of the healthiest cities in the world.

The reports have mounted as more and more foreign medical personnel visit People's China. The staggering turnabout is true throughout this country formerly ridden with filth and disease and lacking facilities to ameliorate the situation. The present orderly, clean, and healthy state could never have been realized without ridding the country of foreign interference, but even after the profiteers were gone, the wretchedness of the human condition remained. The rehabilitation and transformation necessary to meet that challenge are possibly the greatest of the modern miracles wrought by the Chinese in the years since Liberation.

Again Dr. Horn, in describing an aspect of the attack on venereal disease, exemplifies the attitudes and activities that form the substance of this astonishing change:

> Within a few weeks of Liberation, most of the brothels were closed down by the direct action of the masses. . . . [The rest] were closed down by government order in 1951 when prostitution was made illegal. . . . The prostitutes were treated as victims of an evil social system. First it was necessary to cure the venereal diseases which affected more than ninety percent of them and then to embark on their social rehabilitation. Those who had been prostitutes only a short time were encouraged to go home and were found jobs. . . . Those who were deep-rooted in prostitution were asked to enter Rehabilitation Centers, where they studied the policy of the Government towards them, the nature of the new order, the reasons why they had become prostitutes, and the new prospects which

were opening up for them. . . . They were taught a trade. . . .
They were free to leave whenever they wished and were encouraged to organize their own committees for study, work and recreation. Those who were illiterate learned to read and write. . . . When their rehabilitation was complete, they were either found jobs in the city or returned to their native villages where their economic security was guaranteed. . . .

And so we found it in city and countryside, factory and farm, in every condition of life in China. Political, social, and medical measures have combined to control disease and the conditions leading to disease. Although public health was much improved immediately after Liberation (development of strict sanitation measures especially in cities, mass inoculations and immunizations, training of medical personnel), widespread implementation occurred only in 1970, when Chairman Mao put his political power behind his stated first priority: "Medical care must be for all the people."

The social structure was intact. Communal organization was virtually countrywide, and city populations clustered around centers of work. Medical knowledge had reached a high level, though personnel was limited. Public acceptance of medical care innovations was assured by the high morale and enthusiasm of the people who had benefited from other Maoist programs.

Today, when a Chinese youngster cuts his finger or catches cold, his mother doesn't need an automobile or even a telephone. She can get him the immediate attention he needs at a nearby health station. When it is time for her or anyone in her family to have a routine inoculation, medical information, or an eye examination, they need not schedule appointments weeks in advance. They can get such services virtually the minute they walk in the door of their neighborhood station.

Therein lies the genius of the system—organization of medical care from the ground up. It has literally been taken to the people, not superimposed on top of the society it must serve in huge, unavailable medical centers. And it seems to have happened overnight.

The basic unit of this organization is the neighborhood health station. In the cities, street and lane health stations abound, often supplemented by similar units in factories. In the country, every production unit (250 to 650 people) has a one- or two-room health station. These are staffed by at least two barefoot doctors or worker doctors (the analogous position in the cities), who handle all preventive medicine and minor emergencies. This includes vaccinations and environmental health, distribution of contraceptives and education about birth control, treatment of common colds, flu, and stomach disorders using traditional Chinese medicines and analgesic acupuncture, and general followup on all routine medical matters for everyone in the neighborhood group. In case of emergencies, they can perform first aid. Even more important, they can readily detect and refer serious cases to larger medical facilities.

The overwhelming success of the barefoot, or worker, doctors rises from two characteristics uncommon, if not unknown, in the West. First of all, because their practice is precisely limited, they can be trained in three to six months, in large groups, chiefly through practical experience under the direction of mobile professional medical teams. Second, they are always workers in the groups they serve and therefore know its members personally. This functions as a great psychological advantage in a society that has never known regular medical care and in which all trained personnel are suspect of bourgeois tendencies. Not only does it dissociate medicine from lofty, unapproachable elites, but it works wonders in selling everyday sanitation practices and the use of contraceptives. House calls become a practical advantage within these closed, familiar units, and the barefoot doctors' everyday routine includes visits to patient-neighbors to check sore throats, explain medical planning, and provide postoperative care.

Barefoot doctors are frequently women (around 50 percent). They are usually chosen from young people who display interest and capacity for hard work during their two-year stints on the farm or in the factory following lower-middle school. They must seem miracle-workers to many communities who have never before experienced accessible medical care, but as in the case of teachers, their status is not elevated above that of other workers; their pay is commensurate with that of the people they serve, about 400 to 500 yuan per year on the basis of the local work-

Barefoot doctors dispense first aid, routine health programs, and information on birth control and sanitation techniques from health stations located conveniently for all throughout China.

point schedule in the country and usually somewhat more in the city.

In addition to enabling widespread delivery of medical services, barefoot doctors have relieved highly trained professionals from many routine matters, freeing them for specialized practice, education, and research. That they share the universal ideals of medical practice was displayed eloquently to us when the young woman who brought the bottles of medicine for my wife to our compound at Lugou Ch'iao commune spoke of the pride she felt in "serving the people with heart and soul."

Inspiration for the use of medical paraprofessionals in this way is said to have been the battlefield medical techniques of Norman Bethune. This Canadian physician and surgeon served with the ambulance corps in France in World War I and in 1936–37 as a field doctor with the Spanish Loyalists. When he became aware of the desperate medical needs in China in 1938, he joined a medical unit that ultimately made its way to Yenan, then the seat of the Chinese Communist government. There he drove himself mercilessly in bringing aid to the wounded. His life-saving contribution was the small, mobile surgical station near the front lines that made immediate emergency treatment a reality. Lacking necessary trained personnel, he instructed countless young Chinese men and women in such basic Western procedures as aseptic dressing of wounds, use of anesthetics, application of tourniquets, treatment for shock, and emergency surgical techniques. In 1939, at age forty-nine, Bethune died of a blood infection contracted while operating on the battlefield under extremely difficult conditions, but his influence lives on in the mass delivery of medical services through many small units staffed by paramedical personnel given short, specific training. His memory is revered all over China, and his memorial in Shansi is visited by throngs each year. In most Chinese hospitals will be found a large painting of this frail, ascetic-looking hero talking to Mao Tse-tung, who has said of him: "Comrade Bethune's spirit, his utter devotion to others without any thought of self, was shown in his great sense of responsibility in his work and his great warm-heartedness toward all comrades and the people. Every Communist must learn from him."

In training of personnel and in coordinating a complete program of medical care for each citizen, units of the secondary organizational level back up the work of the street and lane and production team health stations. At the secondary level there is great variation in the agencies through which services are delivered—a reflection of the autonomy accorded each region or municipality for developing its own system. In the country the brigade clinics serve approximately two thousand to six thousand people in all types of outpatient care, and the commune hospitals handle minor confinements for their twenty to sixty thousand members. In the cities outpatient care is usually delivered through the factories for workers and through the schools for all children above the age of eight. Factory clinics sometimes offer hospitalization for such needs as obstetrical cases, but generally neighborhood hospitals, like the communal hospitals, are the source of inpatient care. Because populations are more concentrated in the cities, the numbers of people served by each unit are much higher.

Like the facilities, the personnel varies from one region to another. Barefoot doctors are joined by male nurses, midwives, medical technicians, and physicians. Housewives frequently assist these paraprofessionals on a spare-time basis at no pay. How many workers and in what categories depend on need and size of population served. Most small hospitals have several physicians in residence, usually on rotating service from larger municipal centers, although in some cases professionals visit only occasionally. These units, like every medical unit at any level, are supervised by the local Revolutionary Committees under the authority of the RC for their region's health planning.

Services delivered at the secondary level are standardized, for outpatients: well baby care, immunology schedules, midwifery and uncomplicated gynecological surgery, and complete emergency service; and in the hospitals: minor surgery, medical pathology, dentistry, childbirth, X-ray, laboratory testing, and pharmacies well stocked with Chinese traditional and Western medicines. A good system of medical records is in the making, as health cards are issued for each newborn and retained in the clinics of this level.

Our inspection tours of several small hospitals, all recently constructed, convinced us that in terms of basic equipment, technical ability of professional medical staff, emergency services, abundance and attitude of personnel, food, and beneficial care for

[215]

patients, they rank with the best the Western world has to offer. In these centers are linked scholarly expertise and everyday medicine, traditional and modern practice. The underlying Chinese philosophies of collaboration between all levels of ability, trial and error, improvement through criticism, and refresher courses permeate the whole range of medical care.

In China, as in the United States, the most highly trained and specialized personnel practice in the largest city hospitals, the top level of medical organization. They provide the ultimate referral service in cases of serious illness or major surgery for all other medical facilities in their areas as well as the training centers for the medical profession.

Thus, every Chinese—worker, peasant, old, young, cadre or teacher—can avail himself of medical services from the simplest to the most specialized, and the cost is practically nothing. In the country each person pays a token 1 to 2 yuan a year, and all other costs at any level of care are paid out of the communal earnings. In the cities such token payments are generally waived, and the factories assume all routine costs for their workers. When admitted to a hospital, workers pay a small registration fee and about 50 percent of their daily costs, or 1 yuan for care, 0.60 yuan for food, and the same for special treatments. X-ray, for example, ranges from 0.30 to 2 yuan. The remaining 50 percent is supplied by the place of work. If a family is not in a position to pay anything, costs are either deferred or cancelled entirely.

Since the Cultural Revolution, in accordance with Chairman Mao's dictum that medical care should be for all the people, doctors attached to these highest-level hospitals work in rotating service, spending part of their time in the countryside to train personnel (like barefoot doctors), to serve on the resident staffs of outlying hospitals, and to be "reeducated"—that is, to acquire deeper understanding of the life and the problems of the peasants. During our hospital visits, therefore, we inevitably found one-fourth to one-third of the staff on long-term leave, those in residence firmly committed to taking up the slack by working longer hours.

For many doctors who leave their accustomed city practice to serve in the countryside, life is rough and difficult. Shen Shu-chin, the wife of Lee Cheng-li, a former botanical colleague of mine at Yale, is a pediatrician. She received her medical training in the

United States and was on the staff of a New Haven hospital. When she and her husband returned to Peking in 1957, she set up a pediatric practice in that city; she felt that she was doing her job well and serving the people adequately. Nonetheless, when Chairman Mao requested doctors to move from the cities in order to supply the acute medical needs of the country, she asked her husband and two children, then fourteen and sixteen, to permit her to leave them to heed Chairman Mao's call, and they consented. I talked with her in Peking in 1971, just after she had returned from eighteen months in the countryside. She described her life as that of a medical missionary. Frequently traveling by foot or on horseback in rough terrain, she had helped set up clinics, conducted mass inoculations, trained new personnel, coped with emergency situations, all the while teaching the newest sanitation and health-care procedures. She had participated in the manual work of whatever area she was serving. Despite the hardships, she had never before felt so fulfilled as a human being or as a physician. She was determined to return to the countryside, for the need to improve medical care still exists.

Out of such altruism and dedication to the higher ideals of medicine is emerging a vastly healthier nation, and the physicians of China are reaping unique rewards; they are not so wealthy as American doctors, but neither are they so harassed as a group. They enjoy the respect and love of the people they serve, and because of the group organization of their efforts, no one doctor is always on call to answer emergencies at all odd hours.

In 1971 I had the good fortune to visit Number 3 Affiliated Hospital of Peking Medical College, one of four in that city where medical students are trained. Founded in 1958, this hospital has 606 beds and 700 staff members (160 doctors, 260 nurses, and numerous technicians, orderlies, and clerks). Medical specialties include internal medicine, surgery, obstetrics, pediatrics, neurology, psychiatry, the treatment of ear, nose, and throat, ophthalmology, occupational and athletic medicine, and traditional Chinese medicine. The Revolutionary Committee consists of fifteen people: three PLA men, four cadres, three doctors, two nurses, two workers, and one technician, all nominated and elected by the hospital staff. About 140 staff personnel belong to the Communist Party.

The highlight of our visit to this hospital was an invitation to

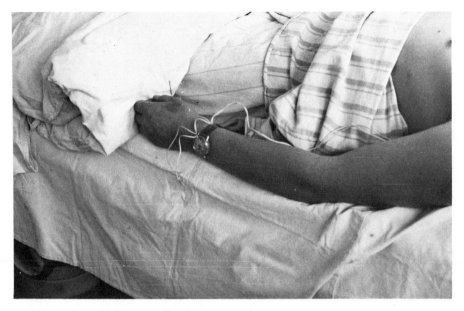

Four steps in the acupuncture anesthesia procedure for a thyroid operation: *Above, a needle has been inserted in the webbing between thumb and forefinger. Below, a needle is inserted in the neck. Top right, a needle is inserted on the other side of the neck and surface electrodes are placed on the chest for the electrical current flow through*

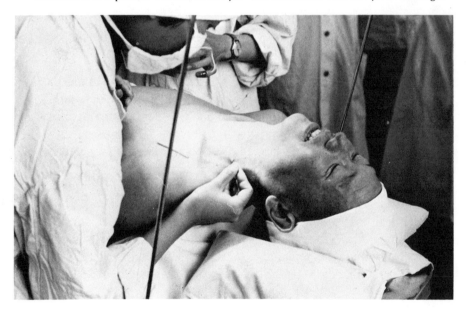

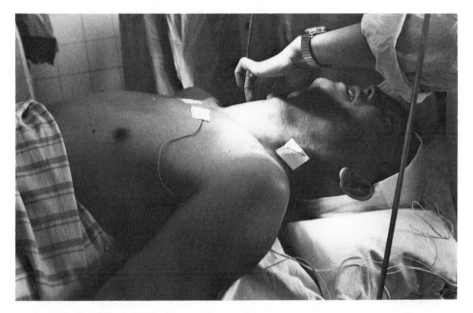

the needles. Once needles and electrodes are all in place the five-volt battery source is turned on, lower right. After a half milliampere current flow for 20 minutes, acupuncture anesthesia is complete and surgery can proceed.

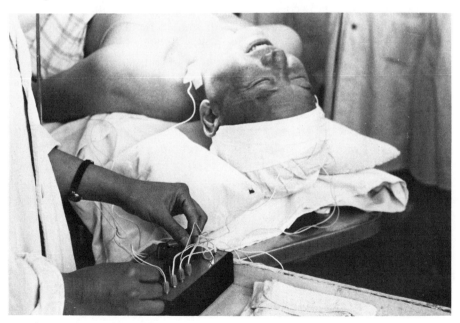

witness four surgical operations performed under acupuncture anesthesia. We were virtually the first Westerners, and certainly the first Americans, to witness such procedures. After changing our shoes, donning white coats, caps, and masks, and scrubbing up, we were ushered into four successive operating chambers. In each case we saw the patients wheeled into the operating room and were able to converse with them through interpreters. Naturally they were nervous about their impending surgery, but all expressed great confidence and trust in their doctors as well as in Chairman Mao, "without whom they could never have been entitled to such advanced medical care." Patients and doctors alike emphasized to us that not too long ago peasants and workers would not have dreamed of being able to afford such treatment.

The operations were for 1) removal of a duodenal ulcer, involving a gastro-entero anastomosis (joining together of stomach and intestine); 2) removal of a thyroid tumor; 3) removal of an ovarian cyst; 4) repair of an inguinal hernia. In each case the body was first surveyed carefully by technicians, who placed a dye mark at the skin points proposed for insertion of the acupuncture needles. These points, usually far removed from the site of the incision, were selected because they were known to produce anesthesia where needed for each particular operation. After approval by the surgeon, the technicians deftly inserted the sterilized needles and rotated them until the patient indicated by a nod or a sound that he was experiencing a tingling sensation, sometimes also described as a feeling of numbness and swelling. For the abdominal operations, needles were placed symmetrically, one or two pairs in the calf of each leg, and two in the abdominal region surrounding the area to be operated on. For the thyroid tumor, needles were placed in the webbing between the thumb and index finger of each hand and others surrounded the thyroid itself; surface electrodes were also attached to the chest by suction cups.

A recent change in the ancient practice of acupuncture that makes it more adaptable for surgical anesthesia is the introduction of electricity. This provides additional stimulation and replaces the awkward mechanical twirling, which is still used when the needles are designed to produce analgesic rather than anesthetic effects. For electroacupuncture anesthesia, tiny electrodes are attached to

[220]

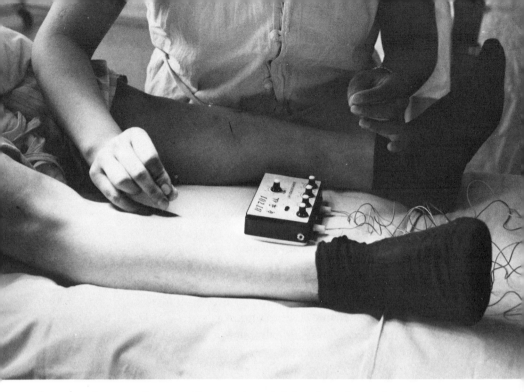

In a hernia operation, needles are inserted in the calves of the legs and in the abdomen near the incision point but are so fine they can scarcely be seen in the picture above. During surgery, the patient (below) is awake and alert; he clutches a copy of Chairman Mao's book for extra comfort.

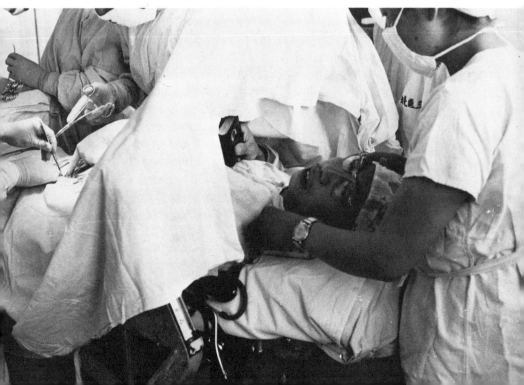

the inserted acupuncture needles, and 0.5 milliamperes of current are permitted to flow from a 5-volt source. When the current starts to flow into the points of needle insertion, nearby organs of the body begin to twitch rhythmically. After about twenty minutes of such current flow, anesthesia is generally complete and can last up to nine hours—long enough for the most complex operation. At this point the current is shut off, and the area is probed for loss of sensation. If anesthesia has been successfully accomplished, the wires are removed and the incision made.

During the operation patients are completely awake and alert and generally cheerful, although the young man whose hernia was to be repaired showed signs of extreme nervousness. Throughout his operation, he clutched to his bosom a copy of the sayings of Chairman Mao, from which he obviously derived the same kind of moral support that a Christian Westerner might get from the Bible. On the other hand, the woman whose ovarian tumor was removed was incredibly cheerful and chatty; in fact, she had to be cautioned to be less talkative so that the operation could proceed without distraction. When the baseball-sized tumor had finally been excised, she asked excitedly whether she could see it. The doctors blotted it free of surface blood, put it into a porcelain pan, and brought it around for her to view. She grinned at it, and after she had been properly sewed up, came up to a sitting position, shook hands with her surgeon, thanked him, and then said words in praise of Chairman Mao.

Over three thousand operations using acupuncture anesthesia have been performed in this hospital alone during the last several years. Among those successfully performed, the surgeons mentioned removal of lung, spleen, eyeball, and extremities. They find acupuncture anesthesia especially suitable for aged and weak persons; there are apparently no serious aftereffects, and recovery is faster and less painful than from chemical anesthesia. This hospital and others like it are equipped to administer chemical anesthesia if it is required, but surgeons generally regard electroacupuncture anesthesia as less complex and dangerous. They reminded us that, although it is not usually discussed by Western doctors, some risk is involved in the administration of a general anesthetic. It is easy to put patients to sleep but not always so easy to restore them to consciousness. A small but constant mortality can be attributed to such accidents in chemical anesthesia but never, apparently, in acupuncture anesthesia. Although acupuncture anesthesia is not uniformly successful (the claim is about 90 percent of all cases), no harm results from supplanting it, in the unsuccessful cases, with chemical anesthesia. In certain procedures, such as Caesarean deliveries, it is clearly preferable to have the patient wide awake and alert rather than asleep and inert, and acupuncture would seem to be the anesthesia of choice.

When Ethan Signer and I returned to the United States in 1971, and related our experiences to the press, radio, and television, our stories of the use of acupuncture anesthesia in the operating rooms of China elicited the most widespread interest. Many people reacted emotionally, either with enthusiastic acceptance or with complete disbelief. Into the latter category fell a number of professional and medical people, especially anesthesiologists and neurophysiologists, who apparently construed our reports as a contradiction of their basic beliefs.

By now the controversy has died down. In an action that will surely benefit the health interests of the American people, the National Institutes of Health have recently convened a workshop on acupuncture. Criticism at this point reflects lack of information rather than acupuncture's rejection. Many Western doctors object to it as an acceptable medical technique because they cannot understand how it works. Only about half the insertion points correspond to neural pathways. How can the effectiveness of the other points be explained? Such objections are legitimate, but the fact is that the action of many common medicinals, such as aspirin and ether, is not well understood either, yet their use is not questioned. Physicians in this country are further disturbed by somewhat mystical explanations of the "miracle" of acupuncture—hypothetical meridional pathways and the balancing of Yin and Yang essences. Although such concepts are easily absorbed in the light of Oriental philosophies, they do not help provide a modern scientific explanation. Moreover, it is certainly true that the use of acupuncture has been developed by nonprofessionals, uninformed about even the rudiments of science or medicine. Alleged to have originated more than four thousand years ago by the chance discovery that an arrow piercing a soldier's body at one point produced a numbing sensation in another part of the body,

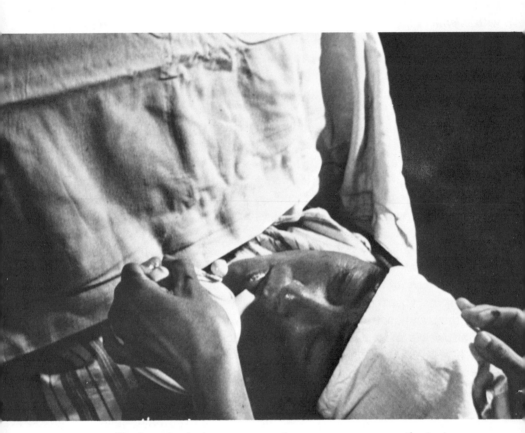

Sipping tea during surgery using acupuncture anesthesia is common practice.

the practice of acupuncture has been developed on empirical evidence, mostly for its analgesic effects. Many people swear by its relief for the miseries of migraine headaches, arthritic pains, and stomachaches. On this matter I heard testimony from several Chinese whom I had known in the West, including Western-trained physicians like Shen Shu-chin.

Most Westerners are astonished by the simple elegance of these needles themselves. Made of varying lengths of fine, flexible wire curled into a tight spiral spring at one end, they can be inserted into the skin deftly with no more pain than that of a mosquito bite. Once implanted, the needles yield no further sensation unless twirled. In some cases, mechanical twirling provides sufficient stimulation; for longer, or more serious, operations, electroacupuncture is preferred.

Originally only about three hundred acupuncture points were described in Chinese medical manuals, but now about a thousand such points are used. The increase is said to have resulted mainly from the experimentation of People's Liberation Army volunteers. These researchers probed their own bodies with needles, seeking new areas that effected the tingling and ultimate loss of feeling desired for acupuncture anesthesia. This would seem to be devotion above and beyond the call of normal duty!

The multiplicity of effective acupuncture points, not always corresponding to known anatomical features, puzzles the Chinese as much as it puzzles Westerners, and the Chinese are quick to admit that they cannot explain acupuncture's efficacy. In both France and the Soviet Union, electrophysiologists have obtained evidence that the effective insertion points coincide with areas of the skin whose electrical properties differ widely from other areas. It is still too early to know if these investigations will provide an adequate explanation, or whether an adequate explanation will be quickly forthcoming. The Chinese themselves are vigorously investigating the physiological basis for acupuncture anesthesia, as we saw during our visit to Peking University.

Similar, large-scale investigations of the usage of herbal medicine in China and other countries may also be undertaken in the near future. This random folk wisdom, gained through the ages by the trial and error of untrained people, has taught that a certain plant is good for stomachache, another will prevent conception,

[225]

a third will lower blood pressure and ease heart distress, and a fourth will relieve the misery of a cold. Increased knowledge of these palliatives and cures may yield benefits for all mankind.

Other aspects of Chinese medicine, too, depend on more study for better understanding in the West. When I asked the head of the neurology department whether the psychiatric techniques employed at Peking Hospital Number 3 were based on the teachings of Sigmund Freud, I was answered with good-natured laughter, "No, no, of course not." When I asked what then did form the basis for psychiatric practice, the answer, predictably, was the teachings of Chairman Mao. Then it was my turn to laugh politely. Our Chinese hosts smilingly replied, "We admit, we are not always successful in the treatment of our psychiatric patients, but we have heard that the same is true in your country." They went on to tell us that, in addition to psychotherapy based on Mao's thought, Chinese psychiatrists prescribe medications, usually of Chinese origin, for depression. Acupuncture, vitamins, and insulin are also used as treatment adjuncts; occasionally hypnosis is used therapeutically, but electric shock therapy is avoided unless no alternative seems useful.

Clinical psychologists are apparently neither trained nor employed in China. As mentioned earlier, psychological deviation, especially among schoolchildren, is treated entirely nonprofessionally by teams of colleagues or peers who surround the afflicted person and, solely by means of sympathy and example, encourage him back into normal pathways of behavior.

A profound effect of the Cultural Revolution has been the radical revamping of medical education. In order to turn out enough doctors to take medical services to all the people, the training period for M.D. status has been reduced from six years to three. This has been accomplished chiefly by the abandonment of much preclinical study in basic science and medicine. Furthermore, the medical schools now select from a much broader base. They no longer require graduation from upper-middle school, thus opening up admissions to barefoot doctors and other paraprofessionals who are experienced but lack the educational requirements. When the doors of Peking Medical College were reopened in 1970, its former twenty-eight hundred students were replaced by six hundred, including 50 percent female students. The plan now is to admit a thousand students each year. Although aptitude for medicine is a consideration in their selection, soundness of political indoctrination according to Party recommendation and capacity for hard work are the main criteria for admission. Dental schools have followed approximately the same pattern.

Since these radical measures have been undertaken in response to the urgency of the Cultural Revolution, they will probably continue to change and develop in response to future needs. Then, too, programs vary from one campus to another. In general, however, Chinese medical students spend their three years in the following way: first, eight months on their basic academic studies, which include anatomy, physiology, biochemistry, pathology, histology, bacteriology, parasitology, pharmacology, laboratory diagnosis, and physical diagnosis. By Western standards so little time would afford only the most inadequate smattering of each. Time during this first year is given over as well to political education and training in aspects of traditional Chinese medicine. Students then receive six months of clinical training in internal medicine, surgery, pediatrics, obstetrics, and gynecology. This is followed by a sort of internship—nine months in the countryside. The coordination of this period with the rotational service term of their professors has the practical result that the students learn through supervised doing and the outlying patients benefit from increased professional medical service. The last segment of training is conducted back at the hospital training center—three months of intensive practice to consolidate what has been learned through clinical conferences, ward rounds, and lectures. The emphasis throughout is on fewer and better courses. These longer periods are interspersed with short periods for physical fitness, military training, manual work, and vacation.

At the completion of their training (graduates are only just now emerging under the new system), young doctors are qualified as general practitioners and return to their place of origin. They are attached to a small hospital and can diagnose and treat most diseases and perform simple surgery. For example, typical graduates should be able to perform any of the four operations we witnessed under acupuncture anesthesia as well as abnormal de-

[227]

liveries and Caesarean sections. They practice a remarkable amalgam of traditional Chinese and modern Western medicine.

In 1972 I fell victim to an intense gastrointestinal malady that resisted all my traveler's aids. Finally I went to the East China Hospital in Shanghai, where I was turned over to a competent young physician. His examination included classic Chinese tongue observation and multiple pulse checks, backed up by temperature and blood pressure checks. Confidently and firmly, he ordered bed rest for three days, a simple diet, no fats, nothing raw, only easily digestible foods. His prescriptions included a vitamin complex and chloromycetin, as well as three Chinese herbal medications. When I questioned the chloromycetin because of possible undesirable side effects, he laughed, allowing that it wasn't necessary; he had included it because he knew I would recognize it. And he was quite right; I took only the other medicines, and my condition improved at once; at the end of his predicted three days, I was on my way to being cured.

If, after a certain amount of time spent in general practice of this nature, a doctor desires more training in a specialty, he can return to medical school. But he must go through a routine similar to his admission in the first place. He must be recommended by his local RC. On achieving that, he will be readmitted if his record has been good.

In medical care, more than in any other aspect of socialization, the Chinese have brilliantly exploited the traditional philosophy of "walking on two legs"—a favorite Chinese symbolization of the practice of fusing the old and the new to solve an immediate problem. By "putting politics in command," they are utilizing the best of every conceivable resource—Western-trained doctors and Chinese-trained doctors, professional physicians and paramedical personnel, Western drugs and Chinese herbs. That Mao's interpretation of medical priorities has been accepted by the profession was attested to by all medical personnel we met. There are surely dissidents, but not in any number. The morale is so high, the success so spectacular, that resistance is bound to be low. Much remains to be done; achievement of the ideal for every one of 800 million in all the farthest reaches of the country surely cannot have been reached so soon. In spite of this, the West could benefit greatly from study of the Chinese system of medical-care delivery and, in turn, could offer the Chinese help in advanced treatment and research. Perhaps further, anticipated reciprocal visits by Chinese and American physicians will lead to just such a useful exchange of medical knowledge.

Because pottery of this design (hsien, a cauldron with a tripod base surmounted by a steamer top) is known to be of the Chinese neolithic period and diverges widely from anything known elsewhere, it has become a symbol of Chinese nationalism. Wherever hsien are excavated can therefore be construed as part of China's territorial domain. Huge copies are found in great abundance in public buildings and monuments.

10

Looking Back and Looking Ahead

NEVER, THROUGHOUT the weeks of my 1971 and 1972 visits, did China's powerful impact on me diminish. Trying to describe the phenomenon of China leads to all manner of paradoxes; old and new, changeless and dynamic, active and passive, surprising and predictable. In contrast to other parts of Asia and its own recent past, China is utterly astonishing in the physical well-being of its people, enjoying their newfound security. The astonishment is compounded by the knowledge that, since 1960, when Soviet aid ended, China has achieved its transformation entirely alone, un-aided by any outside force. Trying to explain the phenomenon at all satisfactorily—even to oneself—remains far more difficult.

China's ancient characteristics—its sheer size, isolation through-out history, and preoccupation with itself—persist, and they con-tinue to make it resistant to outside influence. These same char-acteristics have surely created an ambience that makes possible China's oneness and capacity for implementing and accepting radical internal social change. But explanations for China's rev-olutionary success must depend on some other strength as well.

In looking back at my own experience in the New China, I find evidence for such strength in a unique social rationale that permeates every aspect of society—the group ethic. Developing such an ethic depends on every person's discipline and cooperation and the repression of self-interest in favor of service and loyalty to group goals. This behavior may seem contrary to our understanding of human nature and possible only in a closed society, like China, whose people are not permitted to travel, to read freely, or to experience any other system. But successful social change in China implies more than that. The ordinary people seem to feel that group welfare is identical with their own best interests, thus the internal contradictions involved in keying their value system to group service rather than to personal aspirations are minimized. Evidence for this abounded in our experiences everywhere.

Whenever an individual has performed outstandingly, whether in the army, university, or commune, not only he, but his entire unit, wins special commendation. This is done in the sincere belief that no one ever acts completely alone; the individual is aided and guided by his fellows, whether directly or subtly.

Numerous college students told us that after graduation they would be willing to accept whatever job in whatever part of the country that would serve the people best; they seemed to mean it, although each student must have had individual preferences, perhaps even a specific position picked out. In these same universities, graduate education has been halted and the publication of scholarly journals suspended in a serious attempt to restructure these activities and to uncouple their inherent prestige from individualized glory-seeking.

In the production team at Lugou Ch'iao, individuals already burdened with work and personal responsibilities volunteered repeatedly for extra duty to benefit the group. An example is the chore of arising in the middle of the night after a full day's work in the fields to operate the irrigation system, lifeblood of the vegetable crop. Such outstanding service was recognized at the time of allocating work-points to groups and workers, not only in the approbation of the group, but in extra monetary returns. Yet such labor did not yield returns proportionate to the extra effort involved, nor was the reward assured.

In the same way, physicians comfortably settled at hospitals in urban centers, practicing medicine at the finest technical levels,

[232]

go to the countryside to do missionary work in setting up new health centers, while their colleagues remaining in the cities pledge to work harder to maintain the previous level of efficiency.

Service workers in the cities—elevator operators, clerks at hotels, drivers of limousines, streetcleaners—all perform their tasks with a cheerful acceptance of what life has brought them. Every worker seems fortified by the implicit knowledge that all tasks contribute to the well-being of his country, and that knowledge accords dignity and satisfaction to even the most ordinary duty.

Certain specific social measures have clearly reinforced the capacity of the Chinese to alter and transcend the old system of values. Consider the drafting of every woman in the nation into the labor force. Such a radical transformation of traditional Chinese life style was dictated by the economic exigencies of caring for 800 million people in a poor, underindustrialized society. Today the role of housewife has almost ceased to exist, but women can be found in every possible kind of employment—in industry, agriculture, education, medicine, even the army. Their bolstered status and progress toward genuine equality with their male co-workers must imbue women with a special appreciation for what service to group goals can mean. It has also necessitated a considerable social reorganization; the institution of a new system of welfare care including crèches, nurseries, and factory canteens, has resulted. The effect of a nation of working mothers on the lives of their children must surely be the children's increased independence from familial control and reliance on peers. Inevitably, this provides a greater potential for ideological control by the government and facilitates the government's ability to inculcate such ideals as patriotism and the group ethic in the young from their earliest years.

The extraordinary organization and activities of the People's Liberation Army, too, manifest and reinforce the group ethic as China's social rationale. The motto of the PLA is "Serve the People." Most soldiers wear little red medallions bearing these words—at once humble and proud and a token of more than lip service to that cause. The PLA performs at least three quite different services for China:

It functions first as the protector of China's security and integrity as a nation. China insists on her image as a nonbelligerent nation, and it is true that PLA soldiers have ventured in force outside the PRC's borders only during the Korean War.

Secondly, because of the diversified nature of its activities, the PLA serves as a training arena for new leadership. The activities range from group efforts in medical experimentation and conservation to emergency action in agricultural disasters. The duties and training involved resemble those of a Civilian Conservation Corps or a VISTA-like domestic Peace Corps, and mingling with the people everywhere in their familiar green uniforms, they certainly do not seem like a standing army. The PLA is maintained at about 3.5 million strong, though there is no military draft. In fact, the ablest young men and women vie for placement, because it offers a ladder to training and upward mobility and an opportunity to serve in ways that are personally satisfying as well as nationally rewarding. The esprit de corps is said to be extremely high, and the absence of rank insignia, saluting, and other means of separating officers and enlisted personnel reflects the ideals of a developing classless society and guarantees a fresh approach to leadership. From PLA ranks are recruited not only military leaders but also leaders in medicine, engineering, and transportation as well as factory administrators, university students, and cabinet officers.

The PLA "serves the people" in a third, and less easily understood, role as an agency for political stability. PLA persuasion and force were crucial in the settlement of open hostilities during the Cultural Revolution. The PLA members were sent into production centers and universities to keep order and mediate between opposing factions, but their behavior was circumscribed by five guidelines that bespeak an outlook rather unexpected in the standing army of a world power: 1) do not get angry at the people; 2) do not curse back even when provoked; 3) do not strike back even when you are struck; 4) never fire at people; and 5) just to be sure, never carry arms among the people. In carrying out these guidelines, PLA soldiers were themselves in danger and suffered some casualties. Their efforts contributed appreciably to reconciliation and the subsequent reorganization of institutional administration by Revolutionary Committees. Today PLA members serve on RCs throughout the land. Their service in this capacity forges the links in the chain of command that maintain China's political continuity—and bind it to the Mao regime. But even more, their omnipresence, representing a group whose prestige rests on zeal for service, exemplifies on a day-to-day basis the values inherent in the group ethic.

That the economic measures instituted in modern China have reinforced the rationale of service to the group is apparent among Chinese of every walk of life. Peasants always pointed to the introduction of communal organization in 1958 as the beginning of their improved lives, and factory workers, too, credited their higher production and increased standard of living to recent reorganization of their group work effort. Though evidenced in part because it is linked to their own best interests, enthusiasm for group goals reflects as well the people's sense of contributing to the progress of their country. Lugou Ch'iao peasants were inspired by the thought that more and better vegetable production meant more and better food for Peking workers. Beijing Yuetan workers knew they built the finest furnaces for making transistor parts that China had yet developed; they were proud to supply their product to factories all over their country at costs much lower than those charged for imports. Such confidence in the group ethic and the resultant high morale occur not as isolated instances; they represent the prevailing mood of the Chinese people.

Acceptance of the group ethic yields greater security. This plus high morale equals trust in the leadership. Heady claims these, but authentic in the daily life of People's China. The masses trust their leadership because their leadership has surrounded them with all the material, educational, and medical necessities of life. Their leadership has encouraged "struggle-criticism-transformation," charged them to "Dare to think, dare to act" and "put politics in command," and the mass line has brought these ideas to all the people. The rhetoric surely rolls off their backs, but the essence of it is deep in their minds and hearts because they can see it working. When a peasant stands up at a political meeting to complain that too many *mus* are being farmed for wheat or too little labor is expended in weeding tomatoes, he is listened to. After the disappointing harvest of 1972, leadership wasted no breath in regrets, but criticized the failure of measures against natural disasters, and called on the peasants to struggle harder in

China owes much of her current progress to the prevalence of the group ethic. On a commune near Canton, everyone—young and old, male and female—turns out to carry sand to help strengthen a levee.

water conservation. When a political leader fails, problems are reassessed and procedures transformed. What the masses see is a valid system that functions as the leaders say it should.

The well-being of China depends therefore, as in no other nation, on the quality of its leadership. Absence of elections for high offices means that the people have no means of indicating a desire for change. What is more, alternative pathways through which change of leadership might occur remain unclear. The trusted, successful leaders of today are veterans—wise, enthusiastically supported, but old. More than any other, this situation signals uncertainty in China's future.

Today's leaders look ahead constantly. Though wary of rapid change—they are not rushing toward industrialization, preferring instead to pursue the rural way of life in a labor, not machine, intensive society—they nonetheless warn the masses of impending change. "The next 50 to 100 years . . . will be an era of radical change throughout the world—we must be prepared to engage in great struggle which will have features different in form from those of the past," were the words of Chairman Mao Tse-tung in 1970.

An expansion of this idea proved a most engaging portion of my talk with Premier Chou En-lai. He had been speaking of the Cultural Revolution—"a great going to the people"—and, in response to my query about how that progress could be continued, went on to illuminate what the leadership itself held as important considerations for the future.

He pointed out that the old have a responsibility for instructing the young and correcting their ultraleft tendencies because the young have not had much experience. The older people have to remind them repeatedly of the principles and history of the Revolution. Mao understands this and always trusts the people to correct the dangerous tendencies developing in society. (Here Chou took a copy of Mao's little red book from his tunic pocket and brandished it symbolically.) Mao has thus succeeded in raising the continuing Revolution to a new level of cultural awareness; the Revolution is not yet over—it may erupt again and again in succeeding generations. I mentioned that Thomas Jefferson had advocated a revolution every twenty years. Chou concurred but cautioned that every twenty years was too mechanical; it might be necessary in fifteen or thirty years, or at even more frequent intervals.

That revolutionary fervor can be maintained in a country strong in its continuity with its past, confident of its capacity to adapt to whatever changes the future brings is brought out strikingly by an experience with another veteran Chinese leader. Kuo Mo-jo, president of the Chinese Academy of Sciences, is also a well-known writer, archeologist, physician, and politician—a veritable Renaissance man.

During my interview with him in 1972, I delivered a letter framed by Chinese students in this country on behalf of the Committee to Defend the Tiao Yu Tai Islands. This small group of islands, known also by their Japanese name of the Senkaku Retto, had been included in the recent Okinawa reversion treaty, by which the Ryukyus and other islands were returned to Japan by the United States. The Tiao Yu Tais are more than specks of land in the middle of the ocean. Rich oil deposits are said to lie near them, and whoever owns them will probably be able to profit handsomely. According to my Chinese student informants, a recently discovered deep submarine trench running between the Tiao Yu Tais and the Ryukyus shows that the former belong geographically to Taiwan and thus to China rather than to Japan. The Committee maintains that the United States thus had no right to assign their ownership to Japan.

In answer to the overseas Chinese students' expression of patriotism, Kuo Mo-jo enunciates most eloquently the strength and unity of purpose that characterizes China's present leadership. Here is the letter he asked me to take back to them:

Comrades of the Action Committee to defend the Tiao-Yu-Tai Islands:

I have received your letter, which Professor Galston brought to me. I wish to express my thanks for your kind regards.

Since the paleolithic age, Taiwan has been inseparable from the Chinese mainland. The archeological discoveries of stone axes and three-leg-pottery are of the same type as have been found in Fukien province. You were born and brought up in Taiwan or Hong Kong, but of course you are children

Chinese hospitality with two great leaders in the Great Hall of the People, Peking. From left to right, Kuo Mo-jo, Ethan Signer, the author, Premier Chou En-lai.

of China. The motherland will not forget you, never. She is always waiting for you, she is always ready to embrace you.

The movement to defend the Tiao-Yu-Tai islands shows your patriotism. The Tiao-Yu-Tai islands are part of Taiwan and Taiwan is a province of China. Any attempt to separate them is doomed to failure.

Japan is now at a cross-road. Whether to be a militaristic or a peace loving country is a question that reflects the difference between the Japanese ruling class and the Japanese people. The reactionary Japanese ruling class, whose minds are muddled by the benefits of rich oil deposits on the continental shelf, try to take our islands, the Tiao-Yu-Tai. Our government has made it very clear that China is not the China of thirty or forty years ago. We will not allow even an inch of our land to be taken away. The Japanese reactionaries, if they do not acknowledge their mistake, will only raise a stone and drop it on their own feet.

The new China is only 22 years old. Our progress may not be satisfactory in every phase, but our road is in the right direction. I believe that if we follow this road and work hard, twenty or thirty years from now everything will be even more beautiful and bright.

Let us work hard.

Salute.

Kuo Mo-jo

Visiting China has raised more questions than it has answered for me. It made me wonder whether "human nature" as we know it in the competitive West is the only course of development possible for mankind. It reawakened some of my youthful idealism and made me question some of the deep-rooted cynicism prevalent in our society. Yet the warm glow resulting from my admiration of the working-together spirit of the Chinese masses is dulled somewhat by the uneasy feeling that the present state of affairs might suddenly transform if a change in China's leadership should bring with it a radical shift in direction. But rapprochement between China and the West—together with the opening up of previously closed channels of information—should help buffer the world against too violent a transition. Overall, China's accomplishments reassure me. As a determined and united people that has solved the staggering problems of poverty, hunger, disease, and crime, China offers the world more hope than threat.

Supplementary Reading

Allan, Ted, and Sydney Gordon: *The Scalpel, The Sword*. Little, Brown and Co., Boston, 1952.
A somewhat fictionalized biography of Dr. Norman Bethune, a Canadian physician, whose heroic medical service with the Chinese Communist armies in 1937–38 inspired the "barefoot doctor" movement in People's China today.

Hinton, William: *Fanshen: A Documentary of Revolution in a Chinese Village*. Monthly Review Press, New York & London, 1966.
A unique treatment, from an on-the-scene American tractor expert, of the transformation of the countryside from private ownership to a communal system.

Hinton, William: *The Hundred Day War*. Monthly Review Press, New York & London, 1972.
An account of the Cultural Revolution at Tsinghua University in Peking, based on investigations carried out by the author in 1971.

Horn, Joshua: *Away with All Pests*. Monthly Review Press, New York & London, 1969.
An English surgeon, in China from 1954–69, tells of the remarkable advances in public health.

Salisbury, Harrison E.: *To Peking and Beyond*. Quadrangle, The New York Times Book Co., New York, 1973.
A broad-ranging account of the new political movements in Asia by a skilled and experienced reporter.

Sidel, Ruth: *Women and Child Care in China*. Hill and Wang, New York, 1972.

An insightful view of social services in China by a social worker who visited China in 1971 and 1972.

Smedley, Agnes: *The Great Road*. Monthly Review Press, New York & London, 1956.
The life and times of Chu Teh, commander-in-chief of the People's Liberation Army, together with a detailed account of the famous Long March of 1935.

Snow, Edgar: *Red Star Over China*. Random House, New York, 1938.
A classic account of the origins of the Chinese Communist movement and its present leaders by an American reporter who spent the years from 1928–41 in China, including four months with Mao Tse-tung in Yenan.

Strong, Anna Louise: *The Chinese Conquer China*. Garden City, New York, Doubleday, 1949.
An early observer of Communist societies relates the events leading up to Liberation in 1949.

Index

PLA on, *see* People's Liberation
Army
at Peking University, 192, 195–196
for schools, 116, 119
structure of, 28, 107
in university reorganization, 166
women in, 41, 137
Revolutionary dramas, 155–157, 175
rice, in diet, 76
rice paddies, 61, 94–97
rest break in, 97, 98
rice seedlings, transplanting of, 94–97
roads, tree-planting along, 56
rug-weaving, 145
Russian language, teaching of, 118
Ryukyus, 238

sanitation practices, 212, 217
savings, of peasants, 111
scholars, 185–186
scholarships, government, 188
schools, city:
for deaf-mutes (Peking), 182–185
and mother's work schedule, 169
pressure to conform in, 177–180
primary, 171–180
recitations in, 175–176
schools, commune, 52, 106, 114–119,
169
classrooms of, 115
curricula in, 115, 116, 118, 119
discipline in, 169–171
examinations in, 119
playground of, 117
primary, 115–118, 169
sports program in, 117, 119, 120
teaching staff of, 115–116, 118
schools, lower-middle, 117, 118–119,
169, 185
schools, nursery, 167–169
schools, upper-middle, 185, 188
science:
vs. arts, in education, 187
as government priority, 198
pragmatic approach to, 202
in university studies, 187, 189, 192–
193, 195, 198, 201–202
Sciences, Academy of, *see* Academy of
Sciences
scientific journals, 204

scientific laboratories, 201, 203, 204,
205
scientific research, 185–186
high-level, 202–205
scientists, U.S., 202
sculpture and carvings, 25, 26
seed sorting, 85
seed stations, 106
service workers, in cities, 233
sexes:
division of labor between, 138
equality of, 41–42, 233
Shanghai, 21, 33, 129, 134, 151, 198
Ching An Children's Palace in, 171–
180
East China Hospital in, 228
factories in, 137, 140, 195
health conditions in, 210
repertory theater in, 155
streets of, 130
workers' housing in, 133
Shanghai Industrial Exhibit, 19
Shanghai Lathe Factory, educational
program of, 195
Shen Shu-chin, 216–217, 225
Shih Chen-yu, 7, 8, 54, 59, 61, 75,
79, 121, 123
Shih Ming, 64
shops (*see also* factories), 48–49
Sian, 198
Sidel, Dr. Victor, 210
sightseeing guides, 22
Signer, Dr. Ethan, 2–3, 5, 223, 239
Sihanouk, Prince Norodom, 4–5, 121
silk-weaving, 141, 142
singing:
Chinese opera style of, 157, 175
at work, 97, 98
Snow, Edgar, 201
"Song of the Dragon River, The,"
156–157
Soviet-Chinese friendship pavilion
(Canton), 22–23
Soviet Union, 225, 231
Chinese fears of, 133
collective farms of, 37
elitist system of, 194
soybean, 49, 51
studies of, 1
soy sauce, 49
specialty shops, 155

engineering and technology in, 197–202

factories at, 189, 190, 199–201

factory workers in, 194–195, 198, 199

graduate study at, 202

prerequisites for admission to, 185, 199

Red Guards and, 165–166

reorganization of, 166, 188

student-faculty relationship in, 199, 202

university faculties, in factory and field, 187, 189, 198–199

university students:
  dormitory life and routine of, 189–190, 197
  government stipends for, 188
  group ethic of, 232
  service to masses by, 188
  in work programs, 185, 199

vegetable crops, 52, 57, 99, 106
  and commune criticism, 102

vegetables:
  in city markets, 148
  in diet, 159
  in family plots, 64

venereal disease, 209, 210

Vietnam, 116
  defoliants used in, 2

wages, of peasants, 43, 45, 106

water conservation, 39

waterways, 48

wheat, 61, 78
  bagging of, 92, 93
  harvesting of, 85–93
  threshing of, 85–89

wheat culture region, 76

wheat yard, 85–93

"White-Haired Girl, The," 121, 155, 156

women:
  as "barefoot" doctors, 212–214
  birth control used by, 45
  clothing made by, 152
  in commune work force, 41–42, 85, 91, 95–97
  factory jobs assigned to, 138
  as parachutists, 30
  progress of, 137, 233
  on Revolutionary Committees, 41, 137

woodworking shop, 48

worker doctors, see "barefoot" doctors

workers, factory, 66
  canteen meals of, 151
  continuing education of, 194–195
  formal schooling of, 185
  housing of, 44, 133
  paramilitary training of, 30
  physical fitness of, 139
  political education of, 144, 185
  retirement of, 150–151
  role of, in plant innovation, 134–140
  salaries of, 138
  vacations of, 138

working classes, leadership of, 39–40

working conditions, in factories, 135

work-point system, on communes, 39–41, 48, 107, 110, 232

writers, American, 206

Yale, 192

Yangtze River, 129

Yangtze River plain, 38

Yao Wen-yuan, 165

Yenching University, 187

Young Pioneers, 116, 176